Bali travel guide 2023

"Enchanting Bali: A Comprehensive Travel Guide to Discover the Island Paradise in 2023"."Unveiling Bali's Hidden Gems, Cultural Delights, and Breathtaking Landscapes for an Unforgettable Journey"

By

Esther L.George

Copyright © 2023 by Esther L.George
All rights reserved.
No part of this book may be reproduced, stored in a retrieval system, or transmitted, in any form or by any means, electronic, mechanical, photocopying, recording, or otherwise, without the prior written
permission of the publisher or author, except in the case of brief
quotations embodied in critical reviews and certain other non- commercial uses permitted by copyright.

Table of contents

Preface	9
Introduction	**10**
Welcome to Bali: A Brief Overview	**13**
History of Bali	**17**
Best Time to Visit Bali	**20**
Visa requirements and travel	**23**
Cost of travel	**28**
Packing Essentials	**31**
Budgeting and Currency Exchange	**35**
Getting to Bali: Air Travel Options	**39**
Transportation within Bali	**41**
Luxury resorts	**44**
Mid-range hotels	**46**
Budget guesthouses	**48**
7 day itenary	**51**
Facts about Bali	**55**
Hostels in Bali and how to book.	**59**
Do's and don'ts	**63**

Tour operators and companies	66
Shopping	69
Ubud: The Cultural Heart of Bali	73
Seminyak	77
Kuta and Legian	81
Nusa Dua	89
Jimbaran	93
Uluwatu	97
Candidasa	101
Lovina	105
Amed	109
Must visit attractions in Bali	113
Tanah Lot Temple	113
Traditional Balinese Dishes to Try	155
Popular Local Food Markets and Warungs	158
Upscale Dining Experiences	162
Vegetarian and Vegan Options	166
Surfing and Beaches	169
Scuba Diving and Snorkeling	172

White Water Rafting	175
Yoga and Wellness Retreats	182
Traditional Balinese arts and crafts	186
Balinese dance and music	193
Festivals and Celebrations	197
Shopping and Souvenirs	201
Practical Information and Safety Tips	217
Communication and internet access	221
Etiquette and Cultural Respect	224
Money-Saving Tips and Bargaining Techniques	229
Conclusion	232

Preface

Welcome to the enchanting island of Bali, where vibrant culture, breathtaking landscapes, and warm hospitality converge to create a truly unforgettable travel experience. As you hold this Bali Travel Guide in your hands, you embark on a journey that will immerse you in the magical beauty and rich tapestry of this Indonesian paradise.

Bali has long been revered as a top destination for travelers seeking a unique blend of natural wonders, spiritual sanctuaries, and vibrant cultural traditions. Whether you are a first-time visitor or a seasoned explorer of the island, this guide is designed to accompany you on your quest to uncover the hidden gems and iconic attractions that make Bali an extraordinary place.

In this comprehensive travel guide, we have curated a wealth of information, insights, and practical advice to ensure that you make the most of your time in Bali. From the bustling streets of Kuta and Seminyak to the tranquil rice terraces of Ubud and the breathtaking cliffs of Uluwatu, we have left no stone unturned in our quest to bring you a well-rounded and immersive experience.

This book will take you on a virtual journey through Bali's diverse regions, each with its own unique charm and allure. Discover the ancient temples that stand as testaments to Bali's spiritual heritage, explore the pristine beaches that beckon with their azure waters, and delve into the island's vibrant arts and crafts scene. Delight in the tantalizing flavors of Balinese cuisine, indulge in rejuvenating spa treatments, and partake in traditional ceremonies that celebrate Bali's deeply rooted cultural traditions.

Whether you seek adventure, relaxation, spiritual enlightenment, or a combination of all three, Bali offers an abundance of possibilities. Throughout this guide, we have provided practical information on transportation, accommodation, dining, and safety, to ensure that your journey is seamless and worry-free.

As you venture forth into the pages of this Bali Travel Guide, I encourage you to embrace the spirit of exploration, to connect with the locals, and to open your heart and mind to the extraordinary experiences that await you. Let the ethereal beauty of Bali captivate your senses, and may the memories you create here linger in your heart long after you bid farewell to this island paradise.

Bon voyage!

Esther L. George
Author of the Bali Travel Guide 2023

Introduction

Welcome to "Enchanting Bali: A Comprehensive Travel Guide to Discover the Island Paradise in 2023"!

Bali, a tropical haven located in the Indonesian archipelago, has long captivated travellers with its stunning landscapes, vibrant culture, and warm hospitality. As you embark on your journey to Bali in 2023, this travel guide aims to provide you with all the essential information, insider tips, and hidden gems to ensure a trip to the Island of the Gods that will never be forgotten.

In this guide, we will delve into the various regions of Bali, each with its distinct charm and attractions. From the cultural heart of Ubud to the sun-kissed beaches of Seminyak, the bustling nightlife of Kuta, and the tranquil shores of Nusa Dua, you will find a diverse range of experiences awaiting you.

Discover Bali's iconic landmarks, such as the mesmerising Tanah Lot Temple and the terraced beauty of Tegallalang Rice Terraces. Immerse yourself in the Balinese way of life as we explore the rich traditions, captivating dance performances, and spiritual rituals that define the island's culture.

Indulge your taste buds with delectable Balinese cuisine, from traditional dishes to modern culinary delights. Engage in thrilling outdoor adventures, whether it's riding the waves as a surfer, exploring underwater wonders while scuba diving, or embarking on exhilarating hikes through lush forests and volcanic landscapes.

Throughout this guide, we will also provide practical information, safety tips, and insider recommendations to help you navigate Bali with ease. From transportation options and visa requirements to money-saving techniques and etiquette advice, we've got you covered.

So, get ready to embark on a remarkable journey through the enchanting landscapes, vibrant culture, and hidden treasures of Bali. Let this travel guide be your companion as you delve into the wonders of this island paradise in 2023. Uncover Bali's secrets, embrace its beauty, and create memories that will last a lifetime. Let's begin our adventure together!

Welcome to Bali: A Brief Overview

Welcome to "Enchanting Bali: A Comprehensive Travel Guide to Discover the Island Paradise in 2023." In this book, we will take you on an extraordinary journey through the magical island of Bali. From stunning beaches to lush green landscapes, ancient temples to vibrant cultural experiences, Bali offers a wealth of beauty and enchantment that will captivate your senses.

Located in the Indonesian archipelago, Bali is often referred to as the "Island of the Gods." Its breathtaking natural landscapes, rich cultural heritage, and warm hospitality make it a dream destination for travelers from around the world. Bali is not just a place; it is an experience that will leave an indelible mark on your soul.

As you embark on your adventure in Bali, you will discover a land of contrasts. On one hand, you will encounter bustling cities like Denpasar and Kuta, filled with modern amenities, trendy restaurants, and vibrant nightlife. On the other hand, you will find tranquil villages nestled amidst terraced rice fields and mist-covered mountains, where ancient traditions and customs are still deeply ingrained in daily life.

The island's natural beauty is unparalleled. Bali boasts stunning beaches with pristine white sands and crystal-clear turquoise waters. From the famous shores of Kuta and Seminyak to the serene escapes of Nusa Dua and Uluwatu, each beach has its own unique charm and character. Whether you seek relaxation, water sports, or simply breathtaking sunsets, Bali's coastline offers something for everyone.

Beyond the beaches, Bali's interior reveals a landscape of lush jungles, cascading waterfalls, and emerald rice terraces. Ubud, often called the cultural heart of Bali, is a haven for art enthusiasts, yoga practitioners, and those seeking spiritual enlightenment. Explore the intricately carved temples, immerse yourself in traditional dances, or find solace in the tranquility of the surrounding nature.

Bali is also known for its warm and welcoming people. The Balinese hold their cultural heritage in high regard and are deeply rooted in their customs and traditions. Their devotion to spirituality is evident in the daily offerings they make to the gods and the colorful ceremonies that take place throughout the year. Interacting with the locals will give you a deeper understanding of their way of life and leave you with lasting memories of their genuine kindness and warmth.

In this travel guide, we will provide you with comprehensive information to make the most of your journey through Bali. We will delve into the island's must-visit attractions, recommend hidden gems off the beaten path, and provide practical advice on transportation, accommodation, and local customs. Whether you're a first-time visitor or a seasoned Bali traveler, this guide will ensure that you uncover the true essence of this enchanting island.

As you turn the pages of this book, allow yourself to be transported to a place where ancient traditions coexist with modernity, where nature's wonders abound, and where the spirit of Bali will embrace you with its magic. Get ready to embark on an unforgettable adventure in the Island of the Gods.

Welcome to Bali, where paradise awaits.

History of Bali

Bali is an island and province in Indonesia, located in the westernmost part of the Lesser Sunda Islands. It has a rich and vibrant history that spans thousands of years. Here's an overview of the history of Bali:

Ancient Period:
The earliest known human settlement in Bali dates back to the Paleolithic era, around 30,000 years ago. The Austronesian people migrated to the region around 2000 BCE and brought with them their culture and language. Bali was influenced by various Indian kingdoms, and by the 8th century, Hinduism had become the predominant religion on the island.

Mediaeval Period:
During the mediaeval period, Bali was divided into small Hindu-Buddhist kingdoms. The most significant among them was the Kingdom of Pejeng, which prospered from the 10th to the 14th century. Bali experienced a period of artistic and cultural development during this time, with the construction of temples and the creation of intricate artworks.

Majapahit Empire:
In the 14th century, Bali came under the influence of the Majapahit Empire, a powerful Hindu kingdom based in Java. The Majapahit Empire expanded its control over Bali and left a lasting impact on its culture, art, and religious practices. Balinese literature, dance, and music were greatly influenced by the Majapahit period.

Islamic Influence:
By the 15th century, Islam began to spread through the Indonesian archipelago,

including Bali. However, Bali remained predominantly Hindu, as the ruling dynasties resisted Islamic conversion. Bali became a haven for Hindu priests, artists, and intellectuals who sought refuge from the declining Majapahit Empire.

Dutch Colonial Period:

The Dutch established colonial power over Bali in the 19th century. The Dutch gradually extended their control over the island, but faced resistance from the Balinese rulers. The colonial period was marked by intermittent conflicts and power struggles between the Dutch and the Balinese kingdoms.

Independence and Modern Era:
After Indonesia declared independence from the Dutch in 1945, Bali became part of the newly formed Republic of Indonesia. Bali experienced a surge in tourism from the 1960s onward, attracting visitors from

around the world who were drawn to its natural beauty, vibrant culture, and spiritual traditions.

Today, Bali remains a popular tourist destination known for its stunning landscapes, vibrant festivals, traditional arts, and ancient temples. Balinese Hinduism continues to thrive on the island, shaping its unique cultural identity. The Balinese people are known for their warm hospitality and devotion to their traditions, making Bali a fascinating and enchanting place to explore.

Best Time to Visit Bali

The best time to visit Bali largely depends on your preferences and what you want to experience on the island. Bali has a tropical climate with two distinct seasons: the dry season and the rainy season.

The dry season in Bali typically lasts from April to September, offering sunny weather, low humidity, and minimal rainfall. This period is considered the peak tourist season, especially from June to August when many travelers flock to the island. The dry season is ideal for beach activities, water sports, exploring cultural sites, and enjoying outdoor adventures. The temperatures during this time range from 25 to 33 degrees Celsius (77 to 91 degrees Fahrenheit).

The rainy season in Bali occurs from October to March, characterized by more frequent rainfall and higher humidity. However, it's important to note that even during the rainy season, the showers are usually intense but brief, often occurring in the afternoon or evening. The landscape is lush and vibrant during this time, and you can take advantage of lower accommodation rates and fewer crowds. If you don't mind occasional rain showers and want a more budget-friendly and peaceful experience, the rainy season can still be a good time to visit Bali.

It's worth mentioning that Bali's weather can be unpredictable, and climate patterns may vary from year to year. Preparing for your vacation by looking up the weather prediction is always a good idea.
Additionally, Bali's popularity as a tourist destination means that it can be crowded throughout the year, especially in popular areas like Kuta and Seminyak. If you prefer a quieter and less crowded experience, consider visiting during the shoulder seasons (April-May and September-October) when the weather is still pleasant, and the tourist influx is relatively lower.

Ultimately, the best time to visit Bali depends on your personal preferences, availability, and what you hope to experience on the island. Whether you choose the dry season for its sunny days or the rainy season for its lush landscapes, Bali will surely enchant you with its beauty and warmth whenever you decide to visit.

Visa requirements and travel

Visa requirements and travel documentation for Bali vary depending on your nationality and the duration of your stay. Here is an overview of the general requirements:

1. Visa-Free Entry: Citizens of many countries are granted visa-free entry into Indonesia, which includes Bali, for tourism purposes for a specified period.Nationals from countries such as the United States, Canada, the United Kingdom, Australia, and most European Union countries can enter Bali without a visa for up to 30 days. However, please note that this information may have changed, and it's important to check with the Indonesian embassy or

consulate in your country for the most up-to-date information.

2. Visa on Arrival (VoA): If your country is not eligible for visa-free entry, you may be able to obtain a Visa on Arrival upon arrival in Bali. The VoA allows for a stay of up to 30 days, which can be extended for another 30 days while in Indonesia. The VoA can be obtained at the immigration counter at the airport in Bali and requires a fee to be paid in cash (US dollars or Indonesian Rupiah).

3. Visit Visa: If you plan to stay in Bali for longer than the permitted visa-free or VoA period, you will need to apply for a visit visa before your trip. Visit visas typically allow for stays of up to 60 days and can be obtained at an Indonesian embassy or consulate in your home country. It's advisable to check the specific requirements and application process with the embassy or consulate beforehand.

4. Passport Validity: Regardless of your nationality and visa type, your passport must be valid for at least six months beyond your intended departure date from Indonesia. It's essential to ensure that your passport meets this requirement to avoid any complications or entry denials.

5. Onward or Return Ticket: Indonesian immigration authorities may request proof of onward or return travel, so it's advisable to have a copy of your itinerary or return ticket readily available.

6. COVID-19 Travel Requirements: Due to the ongoing COVID-19 pandemic, additional travel requirements may be in place, such as health certificates, travel insurance, and proof of vaccination. It's crucial to stay updated on the latest travel advisories, entry requirements, and health protocols issued by the Indonesian government and your home country's authorities.

Please note that visa regulations and requirements can change, so it's important to consult with the Indonesian embassy or consulate in your country or visit the official Indonesian immigration website for the most current and accurate information before travelling to Bali.

Remember to always carry your passport, visa, and any other necessary travel documents with you during your stay in Bali. Compliance with visa regulations is essential to ensure a smooth and enjoyable trip to this beautiful island paradise.

More information
If you are obtaining a Visa on Arrival, which is offered at several international airports, you can do so by using the B211A E-Visa, cash, or credit cards.
-Return or onward tickets must include the departure date from Bali.
-Children under the age of 18 do not need to present proof of vaccination.

-Full Vaccination Status (English) and documentation in English for travellers 17 and older.

-If a traveler is completely immunized, PCR testing is no longer necessary for entry into Bali, however individual airlines may have different criteria.

-Sign up for the SATUSEHAT app, then fill out your trip details on the International e-HAC (Indonesia electronic health alert card app).

When you arrive, complete the Electronic Custom Declaration. The Quarantine Precision App will be processed at the approved hotel.

-Extension of visa:You will require a visa extension if you want to stay in Indonesia for longer than the allotted 30 days. For this, you can speak with the local immigration.

-Housing: During your visit to Indonesia, you must make reservations for lodging.

Foreigners must register with the local police or village office within 24 hours of arrival if they are staying somewhere other than a hotel.

Cost of travel

The cost of traveling to Bali in 2023 will depend on a number of variables, including the season, how long you plan to stay, the type of accommodations you choose, and other costs.the activities you plan to engage in, and your departure location. Additionally, fluctuations in currency exchange rates and airline ticket prices can also impact the overall cost.

To give you a general idea, here are some estimated costs for a trip to Bali in 2023:

1. Flights: The cost of flights to Bali can vary significantly based on your departure location, airline, and the time of year you're traveling. On average, round-trip flights from major international cities can range from

$500 to $1,500 or more per person. It's advisable to compare prices from different airlines and consider booking in advance or during off-peak seasons for potentially lower fares.

2. Accommodation: Bali offers a wide range of accommodation options, including budget hostels, mid-range hotels, luxury resorts, and private villas. Prices can vary greatly depending on the location and the amenities provided. On average, you can expect to spend around $30 to $200 per night for accommodation. However, luxury resorts and private villas can go well beyond this range.

3. Transportation: Within Bali, transportation costs can be relatively affordable. Taxis, ride-sharing services, and local transportation options like bemos or motorbike rentals are available. Expect to spend around $5 to $20 per day, depending on your transportation needs.

4. Food: Bali offers a variety of dining options at various price points. You can find inexpensive local eateries, mid-range restaurants, and high-end dining establishments. On average, budgeting around $10 to $30 per day for meals should be reasonable. However, this can vary depending on your dining preferences and whether you choose to eat at more upscale establishments.

5. Activities: Bali is known for its beautiful beaches, cultural sites, and outdoor activities. Costs for activities such as visiting temples, exploring waterfalls, or taking part in water sports can vary. It's best to research specific activities you're interested in and budget accordingly.

Overall, for a moderate budget trip to Bali, you can expect to spend approximately $800 to $2,000 per person for a week-long trip, excluding flights. However, these estimates are rough and can vary depending on your travel style and preferences. It's always a good idea to plan ahead, compare prices, and create a budget based on your specific needs and requirements.

Packing Essentials

When packing for a trip to Bali, it's important to consider the tropical climate and the activities you plan to engage in. Here are some essentials you should consider packing:

1. Lightweight Clothing: Bali has a warm and humid climate, so pack lightweight and breathable clothing such as shorts, T-shirts, sundresses, and skirts. Opt for fabrics like cotton and linen to stay cool.

2. Swimwear: Bali is famous for its beautiful beaches, so don't forget to pack your swimwear. Whether you plan to relax on the

sand or try out water sports like surfing or snorkeling, a swimsuit is a must.

3. Sun Protection: Bali experiences strong sun, so pack essential sun protection items. These include sunscreen with a high SPF, a wide-brimmed hat, sunglasses, and a lightweight scarf or sarong to cover your shoulders or legs when needed.

4. Insect Repellent: Bali is a tropical destination, and mosquitoes can be a nuisance. Pack an effective insect repellent to protect yourself from mosquito bites, especially during the evenings.

5. Comfortable Footwear: Bali offers a range of activities, from exploring temples to hiking to beach hopping. Bring comfortable footwear like sandals, flip-flops, and sneakers. If you plan to hike or engage in more adventurous activities, consider packing a pair of sturdy walking shoes or hiking boots.

6. Lightweight Rain Gear: Bali's rainy season falls between October and April, so it's a good idea to pack a lightweight rain jacket or poncho to stay dry during occasional downpours.

7. Medications and First Aid Kit: If you take any medications, ensure you have enough supply for your entire trip. It's also a good idea to bring a basic first aid kit containing items like band-aids, antiseptic ointment, pain relievers, and any other personal medications you may need.

8. Power Adapter: Bali uses a two-pin socket type (Type C and F), so if you're traveling from a country with a different socket type, bring a power adapter to charge your electronic devices.

9. Travel Documents: Don't forget to pack your passport, travel insurance documents, flight tickets, hotel reservations, and any

other necessary travel documents. It's also a good idea to have digital copies stored on your phone or in the cloud.

10. Cash and Cards: While credit cards are widely accepted in Bali, it's always a good idea to carry some cash for small purchases or in case you encounter places that don't accept cards. Remember to notify your bank of your travel plans to avoid any issues with your cards.

Additionally, consider any specific items based on your personal preferences, such as a travel guidebook, a reusable water bottle, a camera, a beach towel, and any specific toiletries you prefer.

Remember to check the current travel guidelines and requirements.

Budgeting and Currency Exchange

When traveling to Bali, it's essential to have a budget in mind and plan your currency exchange accordingly. Here are some tips for budgeting and currency exchange in Bali:

1. Currency: The official currency of Indonesia is the Indonesian Rupiah (IDR). Familiarize yourself with the current exchange rate before your trip to understand the value of your home currency in relation to the Indonesian Rupiah.

2. Cash vs. Card: While credit and debit cards are widely accepted in tourist areas, it's a good idea to carry some cash for small purchases, local markets, and establishments that may not accept cards. Make sure to have a mix of both cash and cards to cover your expenses.

3. Currency Exchange: It's recommended to exchange your currency to Indonesian Rupiah once you arrive in Bali. The best rates are often found at official money changers or banks. Be cautious of street money changers as they may offer unfavorable rates or counterfeit bills. Look for authorized and reputable currency exchange locations, and always count your money before leaving the counter.

4. ATMs: ATMs are widely available in Bali, especially in tourist areas like Kuta, Seminyak, and Ubud. You can withdraw Indonesian Rupiah directly from ATMs using your debit or credit card. However, be aware of potential ATM fees and inform your bank about your travel plans to ensure your card works overseas.

5. Budgeting for Accommodation: Bali offers a range of accommodation options, from budget guesthouses to luxury resorts.

Determine your budget and choose accommodations accordingly. Consider factors such as location, amenities, and reviews when selecting your accommodation.

6. Food and Dining: Bali offers a variety of dining options to suit different budgets. Warungs (local eateries) and street food stalls provide affordable options, while restaurants and beach clubs can be more expensive. Consider trying local cuisine, which is often more budget-friendly than international dishes.

7. Transportation: Budget for transportation costs within Bali, including airport transfers, taxis, ride-sharing services, and rental vehicles. It's advisable to negotiate taxi fares or use metered taxis. Alternatively, you can rent a scooter, which is a popular and cost-effective means of getting around Bali, but make sure you have the necessary license and insurance.

8. Activities and Excursions: Plan and budget for the activities and excursions you wish to experience in Bali, such as temple visits, water sports, spa treatments, and cultural performances. Research the prices and compare options to ensure they fit within your budget.

9. Shopping and Souvenirs: Bali is known for its vibrant markets and art scenes. Set aside a budget for shopping and souvenirs, but be prepared to bargain for better prices at markets like Ubud Art Market or Seminyak's boutiques.

10. Contingency Fund: It's always wise to have a contingency fund for unexpected expenses, emergencies, or any last-minute additions to your itinerary. Having a buffer in your budget will provide peace of mind during your trip.

Remember, budgeting is subjective and depends on your personal preferences and travel style. Plan ahead, track your expenses, and make adjustments as necessary to ensure you stay within your budget while enjoying your time in Bali.

Getting to Bali: Air Travel Options

Air Travel Options:
To reach Bali, the most common and convenient way is by air travel. Here are some options to consider:

- Ngurah Rai International Airport (DPS): Bali's main international airport is located in Denpasar and is commonly known as Ngurah Rai International Airport. It serves as the primary gateway to Bali, receiving numerous international flights from major cities around the world. Many major airlines offer direct flights to Bali, including Garuda

Indonesia, AirAsia, Jetstar, Singapore Airlines, and more.

- Connecting Flights: If there are no direct flights available from your location, you can consider booking connecting flights through major hub cities such as Jakarta, Singapore, Kuala Lumpur, or Bangkok. Several airlines offer connecting flights to Bali from these cities, allowing you to reach the island with a layover.

- Flight Comparison Websites: Utilize flight comparison websites such as Skyscanner, Kayak, or Expedia to compare prices, find the best deals, and book your flights to Bali. It's advisable to book your tickets in advance to secure better prices.

Transportation within Bali

Once you arrive in Bali, you have various transportation options to get around the island:

- Taxis: Metered taxis are widely available in Bali, particularly in tourist areas like Kuta, Seminyak, and Ubud. Use reputable taxi companies such as Blue Bird, Grab, or Gojek, and insist on using the meter or agree on a fixed price before starting your journey.

- Ride-Sharing Services: Grab and Gojek are popular ride-sharing apps in Bali. You can download the apps to your smartphone and use them to book rides conveniently. These services often offer competitive prices and provide options for cars, motorbikes, and even delivery services.

- Private Drivers: Hiring a private driver for the day or for specific trips is a common and convenient option in Bali. It gives you flexibility and the ability to explore different areas at your own pace. Private drivers can be arranged through your hotel, local travel agencies, or online platforms.

- Motorbike Rental: Renting a motorbike is a popular and economical way to get around Bali, especially for shorter distances. Numerous rental shops offer motorbikes for hire, but ensure you have the necessary license and insurance, and always prioritize safety by wearing helmets and following traffic rules.

- Car Rental: Renting a car in Bali provides flexibility and convenience, particularly if you plan to explore different regions or travel with a group. There are several car rental companies available, and it's recommended to book in advance, especially during peak travel seasons.

- Public Transportation: Bali does have public transportation options such as buses and bemos (small vans), but they are not as commonly used by tourists. These options may be more suitable for those seeking a local experience and are willing to navigate the routes and schedules.

- Walking and Cycling: In certain areas, such as Ubud or coastal towns, walking or cycling can be enjoyable and convenient for exploring nearby attractions. It's a great way to soak in the scenery and discover hidden gems at a slower pace.

Choose the transportation option that best suits your needs, preferences, and budget. Keep in mind that traffic can be congested in certain areas, especially during peak hours, so plan your travel accordingly.

Luxury resorts

Bali is known for its stunning luxury resorts that offer world-class amenities, breathtaking views, and exceptional services. While prices can vary depending on the location, season, and specific resort, here are some popular luxury resorts in Bali along with estimated price ranges:

1. Amandari: Located in Ubud, Amandari is a luxurious resort known for its traditional Balinese architecture and lush surroundings. Prices for a stay at Amandari can range from $800 to $2,500 per night, depending on the type of accommodation and season.

2. Four Seasons Resort Bali at Sayan: Situated in the cultural heart of Bali, this resort offers luxurious villas and suites with private plunge pools and stunning river valley views. Prices at Four Seasons Resort

Bali at Sayan typically start from $700 and can go up to $2,500 per night.

3. Bulgari Resort Bali: Overlooking the Indian Ocean in Uluwatu, Bulgari Resort Bali is renowned for its contemporary design and cliff-top location. Prices for a stay at Bulgari Resort Bali usually range from $1,000 to $3,000 per night.

4. The St. Regis Bali Resort: Located in Nusa Dua, The St. Regis Bali Resort offers elegant suites and villas with private pools and direct beach access. Prices at The St. Regis Bali Resort typically start from $500 and can go up to $2,000 per night.

5. COMO Shambhala Estate: Nestled in the heart of Ubud's rainforest, COMO Shambhala Estate is a wellness-focused luxury resort. Prices for a stay at COMO Shambhala Estate can vary, but they generally start from $500 per night and can go up to $2,000 or more.

It's important to note that these prices are approximate and can vary based on factors such as room category, availability, and the time of year you plan to visit. It's always recommended to check with the specific resort or a trusted travel agent for the most accurate and up-to-date pricing information.

Mid-range hotels

Bali offers a wide range of mid-range hotels that cater to various budgets and preferences. The prices can vary depending on factors such as location, facilities, and the time of year. Here are some examples of mid-range hotels in Bali along with estimated price ranges:

1. Kuta:
   - The Bene Hotel: $50-$80 per night

- The Kana Kuta Hotel: $60-$90 per night
- Harper Kuta Hotel: $70-$100 per night

2. Seminyak:
   - Swiss-Belhotel Petitenget: $80-$120 per night
   - The Haven Bali Seminyak: $90-$140 per night
   - Ibis Styles Bali Petitenget: $100-$150 per night

3. Ubud:
   - Bisma Eight: $100-$150 per night
   - Alaya Resort Ubud: $120-$180 per night
   - Komaneka at Monkey Forest: $150-$200 per night

4. Nusa Dua:
   - Swiss-Belhotel Segara: $80-$120 per night
   - Sol Beach House Benoa Bali: $100-$150 per night
   - Courtyard by Marriott Bali Nusa Dua Resort: $120-$180 per night

Please note that these price ranges are approximate and can vary based on factors like the season, room availability, and special offers. It's always a good idea to check with the hotels directly or use online booking platforms to get the most accurate and up-to-date pricing information for your desired travel dates.

Budget guesthouses

If you're looking for budget-friendly accommodations in Bali, guesthouses are a great option. They often offer basic amenities and a more local and authentic experience. Here are some examples of budget guesthouses in Bali:

1. Kuta:

- Poppies Bali Guest House: Prices starting from $20 per night
   - Bakung Sari Resort and Spa: Prices starting from $25 per night
   - Pondok Krishna Poppies: Prices starting from $30 per night

2. Seminyak:
   - Jepun Bali Homestay: Prices starting from $20 per night
   - Bali Ayu Hotel & Villas: Prices starting from $25 per night
   - Seminyak Garden Guest House: Prices starting from $30 per night

3. Ubud:
   - Ubud Terrace Guest House: Prices starting from $20 per night
   - Tegal Sari Accommodation: Prices starting from $25 per night
   - Goutama Homestay: Prices starting from $30 per night

4. Nusa Dua:

- Sari Room Bed and Breakfast: Prices starting from $20 per night
- Hotel Puri Tanjung: Prices starting from $25 per night
- Mangroove Villa Nusa Dua: Prices starting from $30 per night

These prices are approximate and can vary depending on the guesthouse's location, facilities, and the time of year. It's always a good idea to check with the guesthouses directly or use online booking platforms to get the most accurate and up-to-date pricing information for your desired travel dates.

There are several popular websites where you can book hotels in Bali. Here are a few trusted and widely-used platforms:

1. Booking.com: www.booking.com
2. Agoda: www.agoda.com
3. Expedia: www.expedia.com
4. Hotels.com: www.hotels.com

5. Airbnb: www.airbnb.com (for a variety of accommodation options including hotels, guesthouses, and villas)

These websites offer a wide range of options, allowing you to search for hotels based on your preferences, compare prices, read reviews from previous guests, and make secure online bookings. It's recommended to visit these websites, enter your desired travel dates and location (Bali), and explore the available options to find the best accommodation that suits your needs and budget.

7 day itenary

Certainly! Here's a suggested 7-day itinerary for exploring Bali:

Day 1: Arrival in Bali and Relaxation
- Arrive at Bali's Denpasar Ngurah Rai International Airport.

- Transfer to your hotel or resort in a beach town like Kuta, Seminyak, or Jimbaran.
- Spend the day relaxing by the beach, enjoying the hotel facilities, and adjusting to the local time.

Day 2: Ubud Cultural Tour
- Start early and head to Ubud, the cultural heart of Bali.
- Visit the Ubud Monkey Forest, where you can interact with playful monkeys and explore the lush jungle surroundings.
- Explore the traditional art market and discover unique handicrafts, paintings, and souvenirs.
- Visit the Ubud Royal Palace and nearby temples like Goa Gajah (Elephant Cave) and Tirta Empul, a sacred water temple.
- Enjoy dinner at a local restaurant in Ubud and watch a traditional Balinese dance performance.

Day 3: Temple Tour and Sunset at Tanah Lot

- Visit some of Bali's iconic temples. Start with Pura Taman Ayun, a beautiful temple complex near Mengwi.
- Continue to the scenic Ulun Danu Beratan Temple located on the shores of Lake Beratan in Bedugul.
- Explore the Jatiluwih Rice Terraces, a UNESCO World Heritage Site, and admire the stunning landscapes.
- End the day by heading to Tanah Lot, a picturesque temple perched on a rock formation by the sea, and witness a breathtaking sunset.

Day 4: Waterfalls and Beaches
- Visit the Tegenungan Waterfall, located near Ubud, and enjoy the refreshing cascade.
- Explore the Gitgit Waterfall in the northern part of Bali, surrounded by lush greenery.
- Head to Lovina Beach, famous for its black volcanic sand and dolphin watching tours.
- Relax on the beach or indulge in water activities like snorkeling or diving.

Day 5: Nusa Penida Island
- Take a day trip to Nusa Penida, a neighboring island known for its stunning cliffs, crystal-clear waters, and beautiful beaches.
- Visit the famous Kelingking Beach, Angel's Billabong, and Broken Beach for breathtaking views.
- Swim or snorkel in the vibrant coral reefs around Crystal Bay.
- Return to Bali in the late afternoon.

Day 6: Water Sports and Uluwatu Temple
- Engage in water sports activities like surfing, snorkeling, or parasailing at beaches like Nusa Dua or Jimbaran.
- Visit the iconic Uluwatu Temple, perched on a cliff overlooking the Indian Ocean.
- Enjoy the Kecak Fire Dance performance at the temple, showcasing traditional Balinese music and dance.

Day 7: Relaxation and Departure
- Spend your last day in Bali at leisure, relaxing by the beach or exploring local markets for souvenirs.
- If time permits, indulge in a spa treatment or traditional Balinese massage.
- Depart from Ngurah Rai International Airport, bidding farewell to Bali.

Remember to plan your itinerary based on your preferences and allow some flexibility for unforeseen events or personal interests. Enjoy your trip to Bali!

Facts about Bali

Certainly! Here are a few intriguing Bali-related facts:

1. Island of the Gods: Bali is often referred to as the "Island of the Gods" due to its rich spiritual and religious traditions. Balinese

Hinduism is the predominant religion, and you'll find countless temples, ceremonies, and rituals throughout the island.

2. Unique Calendar System: The Balinese people follow a unique calendar system called the Pawukon calendar. It consists of 210 days and divides time into different cycles, influencing important events and ceremonies on the island.

3. Rice Terraces: Bali is renowned for its stunning rice terraces that are not only functional but also artistic landscapes. The Tegalalang Rice Terraces near Ubud and Jatiluwih Rice Terraces are among the most famous and picturesque.

4. Gamelan Music: Gamelan is the traditional music of Bali. It consists of an ensemble of percussive instruments such as metallophones, gongs, and drums. Gamelan music is an integral part of Balinese

ceremonies, dances, and cultural performances.

5. Nyepi - Day of Silence: Nyepi is the Balinese New Year, and it is celebrated with a day of silence and reflection. The entire island comes to a complete halt, with no lights, no noise, and no outdoor activities. It is a time for self-reflection, meditation, and purification.

6. Balinese Dance and Arts: Bali is renowned for its vibrant traditional dances, which are not only captivating but also deeply rooted in Balinese mythology and culture. The intricate movements, colorful costumes, and expressive gestures make Balinese dance performances truly mesmerizing.

7. Kopi Luwak: Bali is known for its coffee production, including the famous Kopi Luwak, which is one of the most expensive coffees in the world. Kopi Luwak is made

from coffee beans that have been digested and excreted by the Asian palm civet, resulting in a unique flavor profile.

8. Mount Agung: Bali's highest volcano, Mount Agung, is an active volcano and is considered sacred by the Balinese people. It holds great spiritual significance, and the Besakih Temple, also known as the "Mother Temple," is located on its slopes.

9. Balinese Architecture: Balinese architecture is characterized by intricate carvings, unique roof structures, and traditional design elements. Temples, palaces, and even private residences often showcase traditional Balinese architecture.

10. Subak System: The subak system is an ancient irrigation system used in Bali for rice cultivation. It is a UNESCO World Heritage Site and demonstrates the sustainable and cooperative management of water resources by the local communities.

These facts provide just a glimpse of the fascinating culture, traditions, and natural beauty that Bali has to offer. The island's rich heritage and warm hospitality make it a captivating destination for travelers from around the world.

Hostels in Bali and how to book.

Bali is a popular tourist destination known for its stunning beaches, vibrant culture, and affordable accommodation options like hostels. Here's a general guide on finding and booking hostels in Bali:

1. Research: Start by researching the different areas of Bali to determine which region you want to stay in. Popular areas include Kuta, Seminyak, Ubud, Canggu, and Legian. Each area offers a unique experience, so choose based on your preferences.

2. Use online platforms: There are several reliable online platforms where you can find and book hostels in Bali. Some popular ones include:

- Hostelworld (www.hostelworld.com): This platform specializes in hostel bookings worldwide. You can search for hostels in Bali based on your travel dates, budget, and desired location.

- Booking.com (www.booking.com): Besides hotels, Booking.com also lists hostels and guesthouses. It allows you to filter your search based on specific criteria such as price range, amenities, and guest ratings.

- Agoda (www.agoda.com): Agoda offers a wide range of accommodation options, including hostels. It often provides competitive prices and deals.

3. Read reviews and compare: Once you find potential hostels, read reviews from previous guests to get an idea of the quality, cleanliness, and overall experience. Comparing reviews and ratings can help you make an informed decision.

4. Consider amenities and facilities: Hostels in Bali offer various amenities, such as free Wi-Fi, communal kitchens, swimming pools, organized activities, and more. Determine which amenities are important to you and choose a hostel that meets your requirements.

5. Check availability and book: Once you've chosen a hostel, check its availability for your desired travel dates. Select the number of beds or rooms you need and proceed with the booking process. Make sure to review the cancellation policy and any additional charges before confirming your reservation.

6. Contact the hostel directly: If you prefer a more personal approach or have specific questions, you can contact the hostel directly through their website or email. They can provide additional information, clarify any doubts, or assist with your booking.

7. Consider other options: In addition to online platforms, you can also book hostels in Bali upon arrival. This gives you the flexibility to explore different areas and find accommodation that suits your preferences. Just keep in mind that during peak seasons, hostels may fill up quickly, so it's advisable to book in advance.

Remember to plan your trip carefully and consider factors like location, safety, and reviews when choosing a hostel. Booking in advance ensures that you have a place to stay and can help you secure better rates. Enjoy your stay in Bali!

Do's and don'ts

When visiting Bali, there are certain do's and don'ts that can help you respect the local culture and ensure a smooth and enjoyable trip. Following are some key considerations:

Do's in Bali:
1. Respect the local customs and traditions: Balinese people are known for their rich culture and religious practices. Be respectful of their customs, such as wearing appropriate clothing when visiting temples and participating in local ceremonies.

2. Dress modestly: Bali is generally a relaxed and casual destination, but when visiting temples or religious sites, it's important to dress modestly. Avoid wearing anything too exposing, and cover your knees and shoulders.

3. Learn a few basic Indonesian phrases: Locals appreciate when visitors make an effort to speak a few words of their language. Learning simple greetings and thank you phrases can go a long way in showing respect and connecting with the locals.

4. Bargain respectfully: Bargaining is a common practice in Bali, especially in markets and smaller shops. However, remember to bargain respectfully and with a smile. It's important to strike a fair deal while recognizing the value of the goods or services you're bargaining for.

5. Explore the local cuisine: Bali offers a variety of delicious and unique dishes. Be sure to try traditional Balinese cuisine and explore the local food markets for authentic experiences.

Don'ts in Bali:

1. Don't disrespect religious sites and objects: Temples and religious objects are sacred in Bali. Avoid touching or stepping on offerings, and follow any specific guidelines or restrictions given by the temple authorities.

2. Don't use your left hand for giving or receiving: In Balinese culture, the left hand is considered unclean. When interacting with locals, use your right hand for giving and receiving items, as well as for eating and shaking hands.

3. Don't litter: Bali's natural beauty is a major draw for visitors. Help preserve the environment by not littering. Dispose of your waste properly and consider participating in beach clean-up activities if possible.

4. Don't drink tap water: It's generally advisable to drink bottled or filtered water in

Bali. Avoid drinking tap water to prevent any potential health issues.

5. Don't forget to haggle responsibly: While bargaining is common in Bali, don't haggle excessively or push too hard for lower prices. Remember that the locals depend on tourism for their livelihood, so striking a fair deal benefits everyone.

By following these do's and don'ts, you'll have a more culturally sensitive and enjoyable experience during your visit to Bali.

Tour operators and companies

There are numerous tour operators and companies in Bali that offer a wide range of services to cater to different interests and preferences. Here are a few well-known tour operators in Bali:

1. Bali Adventure Tours: This company offers various adventure activities such as white water rafting, jungle trekking, elephant safaris, and cycling tours.

2. Bali Hai Cruises: They specialize in organizing day cruises and island excursions to destinations like Nusa Lembongan and Nusa Penida. They also offer activities like snorkeling, diving, and water sports.

3. Sobek Bali Utama: Known for their rafting adventures, Sobek offers thrilling rafting trips on the Ayung and Telaga Waja rivers. They also provide other outdoor activities like cycling and trekking.

4. Bali Sun Tours: This tour operator provides a range of tour packages, including cultural tours, adventure tours, and combination tours. They can also assist with customizing itineraries to suit specific preferences.

5. Tour East Indonesia: With a presence in multiple destinations, Tour East offers comprehensive tour services in Bali and beyond. They organize various tours, including cultural, nature, and adventure experiences.

6. Bali Eco Cycling: This company focuses on eco-friendly cycling tours that allow visitors to explore Bali's countryside, villages, and rice terraces while learning about the local culture and traditions.

7. Bali Dynasty Tours: They offer a variety of sightseeing tours, adventure activities, and transportation services in Bali. They can arrange private tours or group excursions based on your requirements.

It's important to do thorough research, read reviews, and compare prices and services before choosing a tour operator or company in Bali.

Shopping

Shopping in Bali is a popular activity, as the island offers a wide range of options for both traditional and modern shopping experiences. Here are some key aspects to know about shopping in Bali:

1. Markets and Art Markets: Bali is known for its vibrant markets, where you can find a variety of goods ranging from clothing and accessories to handicrafts and souvenirs. Ubud Art Market, Sukawati Art Market, and Kuta Art Market are a few well-known markets. These markets are great for bargaining and finding unique items.

2. Boutiques and Fashion Stores: Bali is also home to many boutiques and fashion stores, particularly in areas like Seminyak, Kuta, and Ubud. Here, you can find a mix of local and international brands, designer

clothing, swimwear, jewelry, and accessories.

3. Art and Handicrafts: Bali is renowned for its traditional arts and handicrafts. You can explore galleries, workshops, and art villages to find unique paintings, sculptures, wood carvings, batik fabrics, silver jewelry, and more. Ubud and Celuk are known for their art scenes.

4. Shopping Malls: If you prefer a modern shopping experience, Bali has several shopping malls with a mix of international and local brands, as well as entertainment facilities and food courts. Some popular malls include Beachwalk Shopping Center in Kuta, Seminyak Village, and Discovery Shopping Mall.

5. Furniture and Home Decor: Bali is a great place to find stylish and unique furniture and home decor items. Many stores in areas like Seminyak and Kerobokan offer a variety of

pieces, including Balinese-style furniture, decorative items, and handicrafts.

6. Traditional and Organic Markets: For fresh produce, local spices, and traditional Balinese ingredients, visit traditional markets such as Pasar Badung in Denpasar or Ubud Traditional Market. These markets give you an authentic taste of the local shopping experience.

7. Duty-Free Shopping: Ngurah Rai International Airport in Bali has duty-free shops where you can find a range of items, including alcohol, tobacco, perfume, cosmetics, and chocolates. This is a convenient option for last-minute shopping before departing from Bali.

Remember to practice your bargaining skills when shopping in markets and small shops, as haggling is a common practice. Additionally, be cautious when purchasing branded goods and ensure their authenticity from reputable sources.

Ubud: The Cultural Heart of Bali

Ubud is a popular destination in Bali known for its rich cultural heritage, lush landscapes, and artistic atmosphere. Here are some highlights and attractions to explore in Ubud:

- Ubud Monkey Forest: Start your exploration by visiting the Ubud Monkey Forest, also known as the Sacred Monkey Forest Sanctuary. This natural reserve is home to hundreds of Balinese long-tailed monkeys and offers a unique opportunity to observe them in their natural habitat.

- Ubud Royal Palace (Puri Saren Ubud): Located in the heart of Ubud, the Ubud Royal Palace is a historical landmark showcasing traditional Balinese architecture. Take a stroll through the palace grounds and admire its intricate designs, traditional performances, and cultural exhibitions.

- Ubud Art Market: Known as Pasar Seni Ubud, the Ubud Art Market is a vibrant market where you can find a wide range of local handicrafts, textiles, paintings, jewelry, and souvenirs. It's a great place to immerse yourself in the local arts and crafts scene and practice your bargaining skills.

- Tegalalang Rice Terraces: Just a short drive from central Ubud, the Tegalalang Rice Terraces offer stunning panoramic views of the iconic stepped rice fields. Take a walk through the terraces, snap some Instagram-worthy photos, and learn about Bali's traditional irrigation system known as Subak.

- Goa Gajah (Elephant Cave): Explore the ancient archaeological site of Goa Gajah, also known as the Elephant Cave. This historic cave dates back to the 11th century and features intricate stone carvings, bathing pools, and beautiful surrounding gardens.

- Traditional Balinese Dance Performances: Catch an enchanting Balinese dance performance in Ubud. The town is renowned for its traditional dance shows, such as the mesmerizing Legong Dance or the dramatic Barong Dance. Check the schedules at the Ubud Royal Palace or local theaters to experience these captivating performances.

- Ubud's Art and Cultural Workshops: Ubud is a hub for artists and artisans. Consider joining art and cultural workshops to learn traditional crafts like wood carving, painting, batik making, or traditional Balinese cooking. These workshops provide a hands-on experience and insight into the local artistic traditions.

- Sacred Temples: Ubud is home to several significant temples worth exploring. Visit the

Goa Gajah Temple, Pura Taman Saraswati, and Pura Gunung Lebah to admire their unique architectural features, tranquil surroundings, and spiritual ambiance.

- Ubud's Wellness and Yoga Scene: Ubud is known for its wellness retreats, yoga studios, and holistic healing practices. Take part in yoga classes, meditation sessions, spa treatments, or traditional Balinese healing ceremonies like a Balinese massage or a purification ritual.

While exploring Ubud, make sure to savor the local cuisine at traditional warungs or trendy restaurants, visit art galleries and museums, and take leisurely walks along the picturesque Campuhan Ridge Walk or through the surrounding rice fields. Ubud's charming blend of cultural heritage and natural beauty offers a truly immersive experience in the heart of Bali.

Seminyak

is a vibrant coastal town in Bali known for its stunning beaches, trendy boutiques, upscale restaurants, and vibrant nightlife. Here are some highlights and activities to enjoy in Seminyak:

- Seminyak Beach: Start your exploration by spending time at Seminyak Beach, known for its golden sand, rolling waves, and beautiful sunsets. Relax on the beach, take a dip in the ocean, or simply soak up the sun while enjoying the beachfront cafes and bars.

- Beach Clubs: Seminyak is famous for its beach clubs, offering a combination of beachfront lounging, swimming pools, live music, and party vibes. Popular beach clubs in Seminyak include Ku De Ta, Potato Head Beach Club, and Finn's Beach Club. Spend a day lounging by the pool, sipping cocktails, and enjoying the beach club ambiance.

- Shopping in Seminyak: Seminyak is a shopper's paradise with its boutique-lined streets and trendy fashion stores. Explore the boutiques and stores along Jalan Oberoi (also known as Eat Street) and Jalan Petitenget, where you can find stylish clothing, accessories, homeware, and unique designer pieces. Don't forget to check out Seminyak Village and Seminyak Square for more shopping options.

- Fine Dining: Seminyak is renowned for its diverse culinary scene and upscale dining establishments. Indulge in a variety of cuisines, from traditional Indonesian fare to international fusion dishes prepared by talented chefs. Some popular fine dining restaurants in Seminyak include Sarong, Metis, Merah Putih, and Sardine. Make reservations in advance, especially during peak seasons.

- Day Spas and Wellness: Pamper yourself with a spa day in Seminyak. The town is filled with luxurious day spas offering various treatments, massages, and wellness experiences. Unwind with a Balinese massage, rejuvenate with a body scrub, or indulge in a relaxing spa ritual to revitalize your body and mind.

- Nightlife: Seminyak is known for its vibrant nightlife scene. After sunset, the town comes alive with beachfront bars, clubs, and live music venues. Enjoy a cocktail at one of the trendy beach bars, dance the night away at a club, or catch live music performances at venues like Motel Mexicola or La Favela.

- Sunset Dining: Seminyak offers stunning sunset views, and many beachfront restaurants and bars provide the perfect setting to enjoy the magical Bali sunset.

Head to one of the beachside restaurants or rooftop bars, such as La Plancha, La Lucciola, or Double-Six Rooftop, to witness the breathtaking colors of the sunset while enjoying a delicious meal or drinks.

- Surfing and Watersports: Seminyak Beach offers good waves for surfing, and there are several surf schools and board rental shops available. If you're interested in watersports, you can also try activities like jet skiing, parasailing, or stand-up paddleboarding along the coast.

- Cultural Experiences: While Seminyak is known for its modern and trendy atmosphere, you can still experience some Balinese culture. Visit the nearby Petitenget Temple, attend a traditional Balinese dance performance, or explore nearby attractions like Tanah Lot Temple or Pura Petitenget.

Seminyak offers a perfect blend of relaxation, shopping, dining, and entertainment. Whether you're seeking a day of relaxation on the beach, indulging in fine dining experiences, or exploring the vibrant nightlife, Seminyak has something to offer for every traveller.

Kuta and Legian

are neighboring areas in Bali known for their lively atmosphere, vibrant nightlife, and world-class surfing spots. Here's what you can expect when exploring Kuta and Legian:

- Kuta Beach: Kuta Beach is one of Bali's most famous and busiest beaches. It offers a long stretch of golden sand, perfect for sunbathing, swimming, and enjoying beach activities. The beach is also a popular spot for beginner surfers, with numerous surf schools offering lessons and board rentals.

- Surfing in Kuta and Legian: Kuta and Legian are renowned for their excellent surfing conditions. The consistent waves attract surfers of all skill levels, from beginners to advanced riders. Surf schools and board rental shops are readily available, making it a great place to learn or improve your surfing skills. Some popular surf breaks in the area include Kuta Reef, Halfway Kuta, and Legian Beach.

- Waterparks: For a fun-filled day, visit Waterbom Bali in Kuta, one of Asia's top waterparks. Enjoy thrilling water slides, lazy rivers, and water-based attractions suitable for all ages. It's a great option for families or anyone looking for an adrenaline-pumping experience.

- Shopping in Kuta and Legian: Kuta and Legian are known for their vibrant shopping scenes. Along Jalan Legian and Jalan Kartika Plaza, you'll find a mix of shopping malls, street markets, and boutique stores. Discover a wide range of clothing, accessories, souvenirs, and local handicrafts. Kuta Beachwalk and Beachwalk

Shopping Center are popular destinations for shopping and dining.

- Nightlife and Bars: Kuta and Legian offer a vibrant nightlife scene with numerous bars, nightclubs, and entertainment venues. Jalan Legian and the surrounding streets come alive after sunset. Popular spots like Sky Garden, Paddy's Pub, and Bounty Discotheque are known for their lively atmosphere, live music, and DJ performances. Enjoy a night of dancing, socializing, and experiencing Bali's vibrant party scene.

- Dining Options: Kuta and Legian cater to various tastes and budgets when it comes to dining. You'll find a wide range of options, from local warungs serving Indonesian cuisine to international restaurants offering Western dishes. Sample local delicacies, indulge in fresh seafood, or grab a quick bite from street food vendors for a more authentic experience.

- Spa and Wellness: After a day of surfing or exploring, treat yourself to a relaxing spa treatment. Kuta and Legian have numerous spas and wellness centers where you can indulge in massages, body treatments, and traditional Balinese therapies to rejuvenate your body and mind.

- Cultural Experiences: While Kuta and Legian are primarily known for their modern and lively atmosphere, you can still explore Balinese culture. Visit the nearby Pura Petitenget Temple, participate in a Balinese cooking class, or witness a traditional dance performance to experience the island's rich cultural heritage.

Kuta and Legian offer a dynamic blend of surfing, nightlife, shopping, and entertainment. Whether you're seeking thrilling waves, vibrant parties, or a beachside shopping spree, these areas provide an energetic and lively experience in Bali.

Canggu

is a coastal village in Bali that has gained popularity in recent years for its laid-back atmosphere, bohemian vibes, and flourishing surf culture. Here's what you can expect when exploring Canggu:

- Beaches: Canggu is home to several beautiful beaches that attract surfers and beach lovers alike. Echo Beach is a popular spot known for its consistent surf breaks and stunning sunsets. Berawa Beach and Batu Bolong Beach are also worth visiting, offering a more relaxed ambiance with beachfront cafes and bars.

- Surfing: Canggu is renowned for its excellent surfing conditions, attracting surfers from all over the world. Whether you're a beginner or an experienced surfer, you'll find waves suitable for your skill level. There are several surf schools and board rental shops in the area, making it convenient to hit the waves and improve your surfing skills.

- Rice Fields: Canggu still retains its rural charm with lush green rice fields dotting the landscape. Take a leisurely stroll or bike ride through the rice fields to enjoy the peaceful surroundings and capture some Instagram-worthy photos. The popular route from Echo Beach to Jalan Batu Bolong offers scenic views of the countryside.

- Cafes and Restaurants: Canggu is known for its thriving food scene, with an abundance of trendy cafes and restaurants offering a variety of cuisines. From healthy and organic options to international fusion dishes, you'll find something to suit every palate. Explore popular spots like Crate Cafe, Shady Shack, Betelnut Cafe, or The

Lawn for delicious meals and vibrant atmospheres.

- Yoga and Wellness: Canggu is a hub for yoga and wellness enthusiasts. The village is home to numerous yoga studios, wellness centers, and holistic retreats. Join a yoga class, practice meditation, or indulge in wellness treatments like massages and detox programs to nourish your body and soul.

- Boutique Shopping: Canggu is known for its eclectic boutiques and unique shopping experiences. Discover independent fashion stores, bohemian-inspired boutiques, and local designers selling clothing, accessories, and homeware. Explore Jalan Batu Bolong and Jalan Pantai Berawa for a shopping spree filled with boho-chic finds.

- Street Art and Murals: Canggu's streets are adorned with vibrant street art and murals, adding to its artistic charm. Take a walk around the village and admire the colorful and Instagram-worthy artwork that adds character to the area.

- Nightlife: While Canggu's nightlife scene may not be as lively as areas like Kuta or Seminyak, there are still options for evening entertainment. Enjoy live music performances at popular venues like Old Man's or Deus Ex Machina. Alternatively, opt for a more relaxed evening by savoring a beachfront dinner or chilling out at a beach bar.

- Retreats and Workshops: Canggu attracts a creative and wellness-oriented crowd, making it a hub for retreats, workshops, and events. Look out for yoga retreats, wellness workshops, art classes, and other experiential activities that align with your interests.

Canggu offers a refreshing retreat from the hustle and bustle of other tourist areas in

Bali. Its bohemian vibes, stunning beaches, and thriving surf and wellness culture make it a favorite destination for those seeking a relaxed and laid-back experience on the island.

Nusa Dua

is a luxurious resort area based in the southern part of Bali. It is known for its pristine white sandy beaches, crystal-clear waters, and upscale resorts. Here's what you can expect when exploring Nusa Dua:

- Beaches: Nusa Dua boasts some of Bali's most beautiful and well-maintained beaches. Geger Beach is a popular choice, known for its calm waters and picturesque surroundings. Enjoy swimming, sunbathing, or simply relaxing under the shade of a beach umbrella. The beaches in Nusa Dua are generally less crowded, offering a more tranquil beach experience.

- Water Sports: Nusa Dua is a hub for water sports and activities. Take advantage of the calm waters and try snorkelling, jet skiing, parasailing, or banana boat rides. The area also offers opportunities for diving, with various dive sites nearby.

- Luxury Resorts: Nusa Dua is home to an array of luxury resorts and hotels, known for their impeccable service, world-class facilities, and stunning beachfront locations. Many of these resorts offer private beach access, infinity pools, spa facilities, and gourmet dining options. Enjoy a luxurious stay and indulge in the amenities and services provided by these high-end establishments.

- Golf Courses: Nusa Dua is also known for its golf courses. If you're a golf enthusiast, you can tee off at the Bali National Golf Club or the New Kuta Golf Course. These courses offer beautiful views and challenging fairways for golfers of all levels.

- Cultural Performances: Experience traditional Balinese culture through cultural performances in Nusa Dua. The Pasifika Museum hosts regular dance performances, showcasing traditional Balinese dance and music. It's a great opportunity to witness the artistic heritage of the island.

- Nusa Dua Theatre: If you're interested in witnessing a grand cultural performance, head to the Nusa Dua Theatre. Here, you can enjoy extravagant shows that depict Indonesian history, mythology, and cultural traditions through dance, music, and elaborate costumes.

- Shopping: Nusa Dua offers upscale shopping experiences. The Bali Collection, a shopping complex in Nusa Dua, houses various high-end boutiques, jewellery stores, and art galleries. You can find luxury brands, unique artworks, traditional crafts, and souvenirs to take back home.

- Water Blow: Visit the Water Blow, a natural phenomenon in Nusa Dua where waves crash against the rocks and create impressive splashes. It's a popular spot for photography, and the force of the waves can be quite mesmerising.

- Nusa Dua Beach Walk: Take a leisurely stroll along the Nusa Dua Beach Walk, a promenade lined with shops, restaurants, and cafes. Enjoy the ocean views, stop for a meal or a refreshing drink, and browse through the boutiques for some shopping.

Nusa Dua offers a luxurious and serene escape for travellers seeking a tranquil beach vacation. With its pristine beaches, high-end resorts, and a range of activities and amenities, it provides a perfect setting for relaxation and indulgence.

Jimbaran

is a charming coastal village in Bali that is renowned for its seafood feasts and romantic sunsets. Here's what you can expect when exploring Jimbaran:

- Seafood Restaurants: Jimbaran is famous for its fresh seafood dining experience. Along the beach, you'll find numerous seafood restaurants that offer a wide selection of seafood dishes, including grilled fish, prawns, squid, and lobster. Enjoy a delicious seafood feast served on the beach, accompanied by the sound of crashing waves and the scent of the ocean.

- Sunset Beach Dining: One of the highlights of Jimbaran is the opportunity to enjoy a romantic dinner on the beach while witnessing a breathtaking sunset. Many of the seafood restaurants set up tables directly on the sand, allowing you to dine with your feet in the sand and enjoy panoramic views of the sunset over the Indian Ocean.

- Beach Activities: During the day, Jimbaran Beach offers a relaxed atmosphere where you can swim, sunbathe, or simply take a leisurely stroll along the shoreline. The beach is less crowded compared to other tourist areas in Bali, making it an ideal spot for tranquility and relaxation.

- Traditional Fishing Village: Jimbaran still retains its traditional fishing village charm, providing a glimpse into the local way of life. Witness the fishermen returning with their catch, colorful fishing boats lining the shore, and traditional fish markets bustling with activity. You can also visit the local fish market to get a closer look at the variety of seafood available.

- Spa and Wellness: Pamper yourself with a spa treatment in Jimbaran. The area is home to several spa resorts and wellness centers that offer a range of treatments, from traditional Balinese massages to holistic therapies. Indulge in a rejuvenating spa experience to relax and unwind.

- Jimbaran Bay: Take a walk along Jimbaran Bay, a scenic stretch of coastline dotted with luxury resorts and villas. Enjoy the stunning views of the ocean, relax on the sandy beaches, or admire the beautiful traditional Balinese architecture of the resorts.

- Uluwatu Temple: Located nearby, Uluwatu Temple is a famous Balinese sea temple perched on a cliff overlooking the Indian Ocean. It's a popular tourist attraction known for its stunning sunset views and traditional Kecak dance performances held during the evenings. Take in the awe-inspiring scenery and immerse yourself in Balinese culture and spirituality.

- Surfing: If you're into surfing, head to nearby beaches such as Balangan Beach or Dreamland Beach. These beaches offer great waves for surfing and are known for attracting experienced surfers.

- Golf Courses: Golf enthusiasts can enjoy a round of golf at the New Kuta Golf Course, located near Jimbaran. The course offers beautiful views of the ocean and challenging fairways for golfers of all levels.

Jimbaran provides a perfect blend of delicious seafood, romantic sunsets, and a peaceful coastal ambiance. Whether you're looking for a romantic dinner by the beach, a day of relaxation, or exploring the nearby attractions, Jimbaran offers a memorable experience in Bali.

Uluwatu

is a stunning destination in Bali known for its dramatic cliffside temples and epic waves that attract surfers from around the world. Here's what you can expect when exploring Uluwatu:

- Uluwatu Temple: Uluwatu is home to one of Bali's most iconic and picturesque temples, Uluwatu Temple. Perched on a steep cliff overlooking the Indian Ocean, this ancient sea temple offers breathtaking views and a unique cultural experience. Explore the temple grounds, admire the intricate architecture, and witness a traditional Kecak dance performance at sunset, which showcases a captivating blend of music, chanting, and dance.

- Clifftop Views: The rugged coastline of Uluwatu provides stunning panoramic views of the Indian Ocean. Take a walk along the cliffside paths and soak in the breathtaking scenery. Uluwatu is particularly famous for its dramatic sunsets, and there are various vantage points where you can capture the beauty of the setting sun as it dips below the horizon.

- Surfing: Uluwatu is renowned as a world-class surfing destination. It offers several challenging reef breaks that attract experienced surfers seeking big waves and barrels. Uluwatu's most famous surf break is known as "Uluwatu Left," which is a long and powerful left-hand wave. Other popular surf breaks in the area include "Padang Padang" and "Impossibles." If you're a surfer or simply interested in watching the action, Uluwatu is a must-visit destination.

- Beaches: Uluwatu is surrounded by beautiful beaches, each with its own unique charm. Padang Padang Beach is a popular choice, known for its golden sand and clear turquoise waters. Dreamland Beach, Bingin Beach, and Balangan Beach are also nearby and offer great surf spots as well as picturesque settings for sunbathing and relaxation.

- Seafood BBQ: Experience a memorable seafood barbecue dinner at one of the beachside restaurants in Uluwatu. Enjoy a delicious meal with freshly caught seafood, grilled to perfection, while overlooking the ocean. The combination of delectable food, ocean views, and a warm sea breeze creates a delightful dining experience.

- Cave Exploration: Uluwatu is home to several caves that are worth exploring. One notable cave is the Suluban Beach Cave, which can be accessed through a narrow opening in the cliffs. Inside the cave, you'll find hidden beaches and impressive rock formations, providing a sense of adventure and intrigue.

- Yoga and Wellness: Uluwatu is a haven for wellness enthusiasts, with numerous yoga studios and wellness retreats offering classes, workshops, and retreat programs. Whether you're a beginner or an experienced yogi, you can find a variety of styles and practices to suit your preferences.

- Restaurants and Cafes: Uluwatu boasts a vibrant culinary scene, with a range of restaurants and cafes offering both local and international cuisines. You'll find options for all tastes, from traditional Balinese dishes to international fusion cuisine. Many of the dining establishments in Uluwatu offer stunning views, making your dining experience even more memorable.

Uluwatu offers a unique blend of cultural heritage, breathtaking natural beauty, and world-class surfing. Whether you're exploring the majestic Uluwatu Temple, catching waves at renowned surf breaks, or simply enjoying the cliffside views, Uluwatu provides a captivating experience that showcases the beauty and diversity of Bali.

Candidasa

is a tranquil coastal town located on the eastern coast of Bali. It offers a serene and laid-back atmosphere, making it an ideal destination for those seeking relaxation and a quieter experience. Here's what you can expect when exploring Candidasa:

- Beaches: Candidasa is blessed with beautiful beaches, although they may not be as renowned as the beaches in other parts of Bali. The main beach in Candidasa is known as Candidasa Beach, where you can relax on the sand, swim in the calm waters, or enjoy views of the offshore islands. There are also smaller, more secluded beaches nearby, such as Pasir Putih (White Sand

Beach), which is a hidden gem with pristine white sand and clear turquoise waters.

- Snorkeling and Diving: Candidasa is a great base for snorkeling and diving enthusiasts. The waters around Candidasa are home to vibrant coral reefs teeming with marine life. Explore the underwater world and discover colorful coral formations, tropical fish, and even the chance to spot turtles and other sea creatures. Local dive centers offer snorkeling and diving trips to nearby sites like Blue Lagoon and Gili Tepekong.

- Traditional Villages: Candidasa is surrounded by traditional Balinese villages, providing an opportunity to immerse yourself in the local culture. Visit Tenganan Village, one of the few remaining Bali Aga villages in Bali, known for its unique customs and traditional crafts. Experience the village's distinct architecture, traditional weaving, and ancient rituals.

- Water Palaces: Explore the historical water palaces located near Candidasa. Tirta Gangga, a former royal palace, is renowned for its intricate water gardens, serene ponds, and stunning architecture. Another notable water palace is Taman Ujung, known for its grand water features and beautiful garden settings. These palaces offer a glimpse into Bali's rich history and provide a peaceful setting for a leisurely stroll.

- Temples: Candidasa is home to several temples where you can experience Balinese spirituality and architecture. Pura Candidasa is a seaside temple dedicated to the Hindu goddess of the sea, Dewi Masini. It's a serene and picturesque spot to witness traditional ceremonies or simply enjoy the coastal views. Additionally, Pura Lempuyang Luhur, located a short drive from Candidasa, is a temple complex known for its iconic "Gates of Heaven" that offer stunning views of Mount Agung.

- Traditional Arts and Crafts: Candidasa is a great place to appreciate Balinese arts and crafts. Visit local art shops and galleries to admire and purchase traditional paintings, woodcarvings, batik textiles, and handmade jewelry. You can also visit workshops where you can learn about traditional arts and crafts techniques and even create your own masterpiece.

- Restaurants and Cafes: Candidasa offers a range of dining options, from local warungs serving traditional Balinese cuisine to international restaurants offering a variety of dishes. Enjoy fresh seafood, savor traditional Balinese delicacies, or indulge in international flavors. Many restaurants and cafes in Candidasa boast stunning ocean views, creating a delightful dining experience.

Candidasa's serene ambiance, beautiful beaches, and cultural attractions make it a hidden gem on the east coast of Bali. Whether you're seeking relaxation, exploring the local culture, or engaging in water activities, Candidasa offers a peaceful and authentic Balinese experience away from the crowds.

Lovina

is a charming coastal town located on the northern coast of Bali. It offers a more laid-back and tranquil atmosphere compared to the bustling tourist areas in the south. Here's what you can expect when exploring Lovina:

- Dolphin Watching: One of the main attractions in Lovina is the opportunity to witness dolphins in their natural habitat. Take an early morning boat tour and head out to the open sea where you can spot dolphins swimming and playing. It's a magical experience to see these gentle creatures leaping and diving in the water. The tours typically depart at sunrise, so be prepared for an early start.

- Beaches: Lovina is known for its black sand beaches that stretch along the coastline. The beaches here offer a peaceful setting where you can relax, sunbathe, and take leisurely walks. The calm waters are also suitable for swimming and snorkeling. Lovina's beaches are generally less crowded compared to other popular beach destinations in Bali, providing a more serene beach experience.

- Hot Springs: In the nearby village of Banjar, you can find the Banjar Hot Springs. These natural hot springs are believed to have therapeutic properties, and many visitors come here to relax and rejuvenate. Immerse yourself in the warm mineral-rich waters surrounded by lush tropical gardens.

- Buddhist Monastery: Brahma Vihara Arama is a Buddhist monastery located near Lovina. It is Bali's largest Buddhist monastery and offers a tranquil setting for meditation and contemplation. Explore the beautifully landscaped gardens, visit the temples, and admire the panoramic views of the surrounding hills and the sea.

- Waterfalls: Lovina is also a gateway to several stunning waterfalls in the northern region of Bali. Gitgit Waterfall, located nearby, is one of the most popular waterfalls in Bali. It cascades down a lush tropical canyon and offers a refreshing place to cool off and enjoy the natural beauty of the surroundings. Other waterfalls in the area include Sekumpul Waterfall and Aling-Aling Waterfall, each with its own unique characteristics.

- Coral Reefs and Snorkeling: Lovina is a great base for snorkeling enthusiasts.

Explore the coral reefs just off the coast and discover a vibrant underwater world teeming with colorful fish and marine life. You can join snorkeling tours or simply rent snorkeling gear and explore at your own pace.

- Local Markets: Visit the local markets in Lovina to experience the daily life of the community. The Lovina Traditional Market offers a variety of fresh produce, local snacks, and handicrafts. It's a great place to immerse yourself in the local culture, interact with the friendly locals, and purchase souvenirs.

- Spa and Wellness: Lovina is home to several spas and wellness centers where you can pamper yourself with a relaxing massage or rejuvenating treatment. Indulge in a spa experience that combines traditional Balinese techniques with tranquil surroundings.

Lovina provides a peaceful and authentic Bali experience with its dolphin watching tours, tranquil beaches, and natural attractions. Whether you're seeking adventure, relaxation, or cultural immersion, Lovina offers a charming escape from the busier parts of the island.

Amed

is a picturesque coastal village located on the eastern coast of Bali. It is known for its underwater adventures, volcanic black sand beaches, and a laid-back atmosphere. Here's what you can expect when exploring Amed:

- Snorkeling and Diving: Amed is a haven for snorkelers and divers due to its vibrant coral reefs and diverse marine life. The calm and clear waters of Amed offer excellent visibility, making it an ideal spot to explore the underwater world. You can rent snorkeling or diving equipment and discover colorful coral formations, tropical fish, and even encounter sea turtles and other marine creatures. The Japanese Shipwreck and the USS Liberty Shipwreck, both accessible from Amed, are popular dive sites in the area.

- Volcanic Black Sand Beaches: Unlike the typical white sandy beaches found in other parts of Bali, Amed is characterized by its unique black sand beaches. The volcanic nature of the area has given rise to these striking beaches. Relax on the black sand, take a leisurely stroll along the shore, or simply enjoy the tranquility of the surroundings.

- Traditional Salt Farms: Amed is home to traditional salt farms where you can learn about the traditional methods of salt production. The salt farms are located near the beach, and you can witness the local farmers harvesting salt from the sea. It's an interesting cultural experience and a chance to interact with the friendly locals.

- Mount Agung Trekking: Amed is located in the foothills of Mount Agung, Bali's highest and most sacred volcano. If you're up for an adventure, you can embark on a trek to the summit of Mount Agung. The trek offers breathtaking views of the surrounding landscapes, including lush forests, terraced rice fields, and panoramic vistas. It's a challenging trek and best suited for experienced hikers.

- Traditional Fishing Villages: Amed still retains its traditional fishing village charm, and you can witness the local way of life in the surrounding villages. See the fishermen preparing their boats and nets, colorful fishing boats lining the shore, and traditional fish markets bustling with activity. Engage with the locals, learn about their fishing techniques, and get a glimpse into their daily routines.

- Sunrise and Sunset Views: Amed offers stunning views of both sunrise and sunset. Wake up early to catch the breathtaking sunrise over the ocean, painting the sky with vibrant colors. In the evenings, witness the mesmerizing sunset as it casts a warm glow over the volcanic landscape. These natural spectacles are perfect for photography enthusiasts and anyone seeking serenity and natural beauty.

- Yoga and Wellness: Amed is home to several yoga and wellness retreats, providing an opportunity to unwind and rejuvenate. Join yoga classes, meditation sessions, or indulge in spa treatments to nurture your mind, body, and soul. The peaceful surroundings and serene atmosphere of Amed make it an ideal place for wellness activities.

Amed offers a unique coastal experience with its underwater wonders, volcanic black sand beaches, and tranquil ambiance. Whether you're an adventure seeker, a beach lover, or a wellness enthusiast, Amed provides a delightful escape to explore Bali's eastern coast and its natural beauty.

Must visit attractions in Bali

Tanah Lot Temple

is indeed a must-visit attraction in Bali, Indonesia. Located on a rocky outcrop in the sea, it is one of the most iconic and picturesque temples in the region. Here's some information about Tanah Lot Temple and what makes it worth visiting:

1. Location: Tanah Lot Temple is situated on the southwestern coast of Bali, approximately 20 kilometers from Denpasar, the capital city of Bali. It is built on a rock

formation and offers breathtaking views of the Indian Ocean.

2. Unique Architecture: The temple's distinct feature is its offshore setting, which gives it a surreal appearance during high tide. The temple itself is a beautiful combination of ancient Balinese architecture and Hindu influences, making it a cultural and architectural marvel.

3. Spiritual Significance: Tanah Lot Temple is considered a sacred site by the Balinese people. It is one of the seven sea temples along the Balinese coastline, each designed to protect the island from evil spirits. The temple is dedicated to the sea deity, Dewa Baruna.

4. Sunset Views: One of the best times to visit Tanah Lot Temple is during sunset. The temple's location offers spectacular panoramic views as the sun sets behind the temple, creating a magical ambiance. It is a

popular spot for photographers and nature enthusiasts alike.

5. Surrounding Scenery: The temple is surrounded by natural beauty, including pristine beaches, rugged cliffs, and lush green landscapes. Exploring the area around Tanah Lot Temple allows visitors to appreciate the breathtaking coastal scenery and capture memorable photographs.

6. Cultural Experiences: The temple complex also includes smaller shrines, gardens, and pavilions that visitors can explore. There are often traditional Balinese performances, including dance and music, held in the vicinity, providing a glimpse into the vibrant local culture.

7. Local Markets and Souvenirs: Adjacent to the temple, there are several small market stalls selling traditional Balinese handicrafts, clothing, and souvenirs. Visitors can shop

for unique items, including local artwork, clothing, and decorative pieces.

8. Accessible during Low Tide: During low tide, it is possible to walk to the base of the temple and explore the area up close. This allows visitors to appreciate the architectural details and experience the spiritual atmosphere of the temple.

When visiting Tanah Lot Temple, it is essential to dress respectfully and follow any guidelines or restrictions set by the temple authorities. It can get crowded, especially during peak tourist seasons, so arriving early or visiting during weekdays may help avoid larger crowds.

Note: It's always a good idea to check the latest information and guidelines regarding the visiting hours and access to Tanah Lot Temple before planning your visit, as there may be changes or restrictions due to local circumstances or ceremonies.

Tegallalang Rice Terraces is another must-visit attraction in Bali, known for its stunning landscapes and traditional agricultural practices. Here's some information about Tegallalang Rice Terraces:

1. Location: Tegallalang Rice Terraces are located in the village of Tegallalang, which is about 10 kilometers north of Ubud, one of Bali's cultural hubs. The terraces are nestled in the lush green hills of central Bali.

2. Scenic Beauty: The rice terraces in Tegallalang are renowned for their breathtaking natural beauty. The tiered rice fields create a picturesque landscape with vibrant shades of green, forming a stunning patchwork against the backdrop of the surrounding hills.

3. Cultural Significance: The terraced rice fields of Bali are not only visually captivating

but also hold cultural and agricultural importance. They represent the traditional Balinese Subak irrigation system, which is a UNESCO World Heritage site. The Subak system highlights the harmonious relationship between humans, water, and land in rice cultivation.

4. Trekking and Exploration: Tegallalang Rice Terraces offer visitors the opportunity to explore the area by foot. There are pathways and trails that lead through the rice fields, allowing you to immerse yourself in the natural beauty and experience the tranquility of the surroundings. Trekking through the terraces also provides unique photo opportunities.

5. Cultural Experiences: While exploring the rice terraces, you may encounter local farmers working in the fields. This offers a chance to interact with them, learn about their traditional farming techniques, and gain insights into Balinese agricultural practices.

You can also visit nearby villages to discover the local crafts, traditional art, and cultural heritage.

6. Cafes and Restaurants: Along the ridge of Tegallalang Rice Terraces, there are several cafes and restaurants offering panoramic views of the terraced landscapes. Enjoying a meal or a cup of coffee while overlooking the scenic beauty can be a memorable experience.

7. Souvenir Shopping: At various points near the rice terraces, you'll find small shops and market stalls selling locally made handicrafts, artwork, and souvenirs. It's an excellent opportunity to purchase unique Balinese items and support local artisans.

8. Sunrise and Sunset Views: Tegallalang Rice Terraces are particularly enchanting during sunrise and sunset. The soft golden light cast on the terraces creates a magical atmosphere. Consider visiting early in the

morning or late afternoon to witness the breathtaking colors and capture stunning photographs.

When visiting Tegallalang Rice Terraces, it's advisable to wear comfortable shoes and bring along water and sun protection, as the terrain can be uneven, and the sun can be intense. Exploring the terraces may involve some walking or hiking, so it's important to be prepared accordingly.

Note: As with any tourist destination, it's recommended to check the latest information and guidelines regarding visiting hours, entrance fees, and any local regulations before planning your trip to Tegallalang Rice Terraces.

Mount Batur and Lake Batur
 are two interconnected natural attractions in Bali that are definitely worth visiting. Here's some information about both:

1. Mount Batur: Mount Batur is an active volcano located in the Kintamani District, about 60 kilometers northeast of Denpasar. It stands at an elevation of 1,717 meters (5,633 feet) and offers a rewarding hiking experience for adventurous travelers. The sunrise trek to the summit of Mount Batur is particularly popular, as it provides stunning panoramic views of the surrounding landscapes.

2. Sunrise Trek: The sunrise trek to Mount Batur usually starts in the early morning hours, allowing hikers to reach the summit in time for sunrise. The trek is moderately challenging, taking around two to three hours to complete. It involves hiking through volcanic landscapes, lush forests, and rocky terrains. The rewarding view from the summit includes a panoramic vista of the surrounding mountains, Lake Batur, and even Mount Agung in the distance.

3. Lake Batur: Lake Batur is the largest lake in Bali and is situated in the caldera of Mount Batur. The lake is renowned for its scenic beauty, serene atmosphere, and opportunities for various water activities. It covers an area of about 16 square kilometers (6.2 square miles) and is surrounded by lush greenery and picturesque villages.

4. Boat Tours: Taking a boat tour on Lake Batur is a popular activity for visitors. You can hire a traditional wooden boat, known as a jukung, and explore the lake while enjoying the peaceful surroundings. The boat tours often include stops at Trunyan Village, famous for its unique burial traditions, and Toya Bungkah Hot Springs, where you can relax in natural hot springs.

5. Hot Springs: Toya Bungkah Hot Springs, located near the shores of Lake Batur, is a great place to unwind after a trek or boat tour. The natural hot springs offer a soothing

and therapeutic experience. You can enjoy the warm waters while taking in the views of the lake and the surrounding volcanic landscape.

6. Cultural Visits: The area around Mount Batur and Lake Batur is also known for its cultural attractions. There are several traditional villages nearby, such as Trunyan, where you can witness authentic Balinese customs and rituals. These cultural visits provide insights into the local way of life and add depth to your experience.

7. Volcanic Geology: Exploring the volcanic geology of Mount Batur and the surrounding area is a fascinating experience. You can observe volcanic cones, lava fields, and even steam vents on your hike or boat tour. The volcanic landscape creates a unique and awe-inspiring environment.

When planning a visit to Mount Batur and Lake Batur, it's important to consider the weather conditions and consult with local guides or tour operators for the most up-to-date information on hiking conditions and safety precautions. It's also recommended to wear suitable hiking gear, carry enough water, and be prepared for changing weather conditions during the trek.

Note: As with any outdoor activity, it's advisable to follow any safety guidelines and regulations set by local authorities to ensure a safe and enjoyable experience.

The Sacred Monkey Forest Sanctuary, also known as the Ubud Monkey Forest, is a popular tourist attraction located in the heart of Ubud, Bali. Here's some information about the sanctuary and what makes it worth visiting:

1. Location and Setting: The Sacred Monkey Forest Sanctuary is situated within the village of Padangtegal, which is about 3

kilometers southwest of central Ubud. The sanctuary is set amidst a lush forest, encompassing approximately 27 acres of land, making it a unique and natural environment for the resident macaque monkeys.

2. Cultural and Spiritual Significance: The monkey forest holds great cultural and spiritual significance to the local community. It is a sacred site and is home to three ancient Hindu temples—Pura Dalem Agung Padangtegal, Pura Beji, and Pura Prajapati. The temples are actively used by the locals for worship and ceremonies, adding to the sanctity of the place.

3. Macaque Monkey Population: The sanctuary is home to over 700 long-tailed macaque monkeys (Macaca fascicularis). The monkeys are free to roam within the forest and have become accustomed to the presence of visitors. Observing and

interacting with the monkeys is a unique and entertaining experience for many visitors.

4. Up-Close Monkey Interactions: Visitors to the sanctuary can observe the monkeys in their natural habitat and witness their playful behavior up close. It's possible to see the monkeys swinging from trees, grooming each other, or even interacting with visitors. However, it's important to follow the guidelines provided by the sanctuary to ensure the safety and well-being of both visitors and monkeys.

5. Conservation and Education: The Sacred Monkey Forest Sanctuary has a strong focus on conservation and education. The sanctuary aims to preserve the natural habitat of the monkeys and educate visitors about their importance in Balinese culture and the overall ecosystem. There are information boards and guided tours available to learn more about the monkeys and the sanctuary's conservation efforts.

6. Scenic Walks and Ancient Trees: Walking through the sanctuary allows visitors to appreciate the beauty of the forest and its ancient trees. Some of the trees are several centuries old and are considered sacred. The paths wind through the lush greenery, providing a serene and picturesque environment.

7. Unique Photography Opportunities: The Sacred Monkey Forest Sanctuary offers numerous opportunities for unique and memorable photographs. The monkeys, temples, and natural surroundings provide interesting subjects and backdrops for capturing beautiful images.

8. Souvenir Shops and Cafés: Adjacent to the sanctuary, there are several shops and cafés where visitors can relax, grab a snack, or purchase souvenirs. These establishments offer a chance to take a

break and immerse yourself in the ambiance of Ubud.

While visiting the Sacred Monkey Forest Sanctuary, it's important to follow the guidelines provided by the sanctuary management to ensure your safety and the well-being of the monkeys. Avoid feeding the monkeys or carrying any items that may attract their attention, as they are wild animals and may exhibit unpredictable behavior.

Note: It's advisable to check the latest information and guidelines regarding visiting hours and regulations before planning your trip to the Sacred Monkey Forest Sanctuary, as there may be changes or restrictions due to local circumstances or to protect the welfare of the monkeys.

Uluwatu Temple and the Kecak Dance are two significant cultural attractions in Bali that are often visited together. Here's some information about both:

1. Uluwatu Temple: Uluwatu Temple, also known as Pura Luhur Uluwatu, is a magnificent cliffside temple located on the southwestern tip of Bali's Bukit Peninsula. Perched on a steep cliff approximately 70 meters above the Indian Ocean, the temple offers breathtaking panoramic views of the ocean and stunning sunsets. It is dedicated to the Balinese sea gods and is considered one of the island's six most important temples.

2. Architectural Marvel: Uluwatu Temple showcases traditional Balinese architecture and intricate stone carvings. The temple's setting, perched on the edge of a cliff, adds to its dramatic appeal. Visitors can explore the temple complex, which includes several small shrines and pavilions, as well as enjoy the beautiful coastal scenery.

3. Cultural Significance: Uluwatu Temple holds great cultural and spiritual significance in Balinese Hinduism. It is believed to guard the island against evil spirits that may come from the sea. Visitors can witness traditional rituals and ceremonies held at the temple, providing a glimpse into Balinese spirituality and religious practices.

4. Kecak Dance: The Kecak Dance is a captivating traditional Balinese dance performance that is often staged at Uluwatu Temple during sunset. The dance tells the story from the Hindu epic Ramayana, focusing on the battle between Prince Rama and the evil King Ravana. What makes the Kecak Dance unique is the absence of musical instruments; instead, a large group of male dancers forms a circle and provides the music with their rhythmic chanting of "cak" sounds.

5. Sunset Views: Watching the Kecak Dance at Uluwatu Temple during sunset

adds to the magical experience. The temple's cliffside location provides a stunning backdrop as the sun dips below the horizon, casting a warm glow over the temple and the surrounding ocean. It's advisable to arrive early to secure a good spot and enjoy the sunset views.

6. Traditional Balinese Performances: Uluwatu Temple often hosts other traditional Balinese performances alongside the Kecak Dance. These can include classical dance forms like the Legong or Barong Dance, showcasing the rich cultural heritage of Bali. Attending these performances allows visitors to immerse themselves in the beauty of Balinese arts and traditions.

7. Monkey Interactions: Similar to the Sacred Monkey Forest Sanctuary, Uluwatu Temple is also home to a population of monkeys. Visitors may encounter monkeys in and around the temple grounds. It's important to be cautious and keep personal

belongings secure, as monkeys can be mischievous and may attempt to snatch items.

8. Dress Code: As with any temple in Bali, it's important to dress respectfully when visiting Uluwatu Temple. Both men and women should cover their legs with a sarong (provided at the entrance) and wear a sash around their waist as a mark of respect.

Note: It's advisable to check the performance schedules and any specific guidelines or restrictions before planning your visit to Uluwatu Temple and the Kecak Dance, as there may be changes or variations in the performance timings or other considerations due to local circumstances or ceremonies.

Goa Gajah
also known as the Elephant Cave, is an ancient archaeological site and temple located on the island of Bali. Here's some information about Goa Gajah:

1. Location: Goa Gajah is situated in the Bedulu village, approximately 6 kilometres southeast of Ubud, one of Bali's cultural centres. The site is easily accessible and is often included in itineraries for those exploring the Ubud area.

2. Historical Significance: Goa Gajah dates back to the 9th century and holds historical and cultural significance. It is believed to have served as a sanctuary for meditation and spiritual practices. The site was rediscovered in the 20th century and has since become a popular tourist attraction.

3. Architecture and Art: The highlight of Goa Gajah is its distinctive entrance, featuring a carved stone facade with menacing faces.

These carvings depict demonic creatures and mythical figures from Balinese folklore. Inside the cave, there are niches and statues representing Hindu deities and Buddhist influences, showcasing the syncretism of religious beliefs in Bali.

4. Cave Exploration: Visitors can enter the cave and explore its interior. The cave itself is relatively small, with narrow passages leading to various chambers. While the main chamber is not very deep, it still holds an air of mystery and ancient ambiance. Exploring the cave allows visitors to appreciate the unique architecture and the spiritual significance associated with the site.

5. Surrounding Grounds: Beyond the cave, Goa Gajah is set amidst lush greenery and serene gardens. Strolling through the surrounding grounds provides a tranquil and scenic experience. You can admire the well-maintained landscapes, including lotus

ponds, stone carvings, and statues, which add to the overall ambiance of the site.

6. Sacred Pools: Adjacent to the cave, there are sacred pools where visitors can cleanse themselves in the holy waters. These pools are believed to have spiritual and purifying properties. Many visitors participate in the water ritual as a form of spiritual experience or to seek blessings.

7. Temple Complex: Goa Gajah is not just a cave but also a temple complex. Apart from the main cave, there are several other shrines and pavilions scattered throughout the site. These structures are used for worship and ceremonial activities. Exploring the temple complex provides insights into the religious practices and rituals of the Balinese people.

8. Cultural Experience: Visiting Goa Gajah offers a glimpse into Balinese culture and spirituality. The site provides an opportunity

to witness and learn about the blend of Hindu and Buddhist traditions in Bali. It's common to see locals engaged in prayer and rituals, contributing to the cultural ambiance of the place.

When visiting Goa Gajah, it's advisable to dress respectfully, covering your shoulders and legs. Sarongs and sashes are often available for rent at the entrance. Additionally, it's recommended to bring comfortable footwear as the site involves walking and exploring different areas.

Note: It's always a good idea to check the latest information and guidelines regarding visiting hours, entrance fees, and any local regulations before planning your visit to Goa Gajah (Elephant Cave), as there may be changes or restrictions due to local circumstances or ceremonies.

Tirta Empul Temple, also known as the Holy Water Temple, is a significant Hindu temple located in the village of Tampaksiring, approximately 15 kilometers northeast of Ubud in Bali. Here's some information about Tirta Empul Temple:

1. Spiritual Significance: Tirta Empul Temple is one of the most important and sacred water temples in Bali. It holds deep spiritual significance for Balinese Hindus as it is believed to have been created by the god Indra and possesses purifying powers. The temple is dedicated to Vishnu, one of the principal deities in Hinduism.

2. Holy Spring: The temple is renowned for its natural spring, which is believed to be a source of holy water. The spring feeds into various purification pools and bathing areas within the temple complex. Balinese Hindus visit Tirta Empul to partake in a ritual bathing experience to cleanse themselves spiritually and seek blessings.

3. Ritual Bathing: Visitors to Tirta Empul have the opportunity to participate in the ritual bathing ceremony. The process involves following a specific sequence of bathing in each of the 13 fountains within the main pool. The water is considered to have curative and purifying properties, and the ritual is seen as a way to cleanse the body, mind, and soul.

4. Architecture and Layout: Tirta Empul Temple showcases traditional Balinese temple architecture. The complex consists of several courtyards, pavilions, and shrines. The buildings feature intricate stone carvings and ornate Balinese gateways (candi bentar). The temple's serene and picturesque setting adds to its allure.

5. Pura Taman Suci Complex: In addition to the main Tirta Empul Temple, there is a larger complex known as Pura Taman Suci. This complex consists of several temples,

including Pura Jaba Tengah, Pura Jeroan, and Pura Dalem. Each temple has its own unique significance and is used for different ceremonies and rituals.

6. Cultural Experience: Visiting Tirta Empul Temple provides an immersive cultural experience. You can observe the locals engaging in prayer, making offerings, and participating in rituals. Witnessing these practices allows visitors to gain a deeper understanding of Balinese Hinduism and the importance of water purification in their religious traditions.

7. Scenic Surroundings: The temple is situated amidst lush greenery, with rice terraces and a flowing river adding to the natural beauty of the surroundings. It offers a serene and tranquil atmosphere, ideal for contemplation and reflection.

8. Local Market and Souvenirs: Near the temple, there are small markets and shops

where you can find traditional Balinese handicrafts, souvenirs, and offerings for your own temple visit. It's an opportunity to browse and purchase unique items to commemorate your visit.

When visiting Tirta Empul Temple, it's important to dress respectfully, covering your shoulders and legs. Sarongs and sashes are available for rent at the entrance. It's also customary to make a donation at the temple.

Note: It's advisable to check the latest information and guidelines regarding visiting hours, entrance fees, and any local regulations before planning your visit to Tirta Empul Temple, as there may be changes or restrictions due to local circumstances or ceremonies.

Bali Safari and Marine Park
is a popular theme park and conservation area located in Gianyar, Bali. Here's some information about Bali Safari and Marine Park:

1. Wildlife Experience: Bali Safari and Marine Park offers visitors a unique opportunity to observe and interact with a wide range of animal species. The park is home to over 100 species of animals from different parts of the world, including elephants, tigers, lions, zebras, orangutans, giraffes, and many more. Visitors can embark on a safari journey through the park to see these animals up close in their natural habitats.

2. Safari Journey: The main attraction of the park is the Safari Journey, a guided tour that takes visitors through different habitats to see the animals in a close-to-natural environment. Visitors board safari vehicles

and journey through the park's landscape, coming face to face with animals such as rhinos, zebras, and lions. It's a thrilling and educational experience that allows for an immersive wildlife encounter.

3. Animal Shows and Performances: Bali Safari and Marine Park features a variety of animal shows and performances throughout the day. These include elephant talent shows, tiger shows, and cultural performances showcasing the traditional dances and music of Bali. The shows provide entertainment and an opportunity to learn more about the animals and Balinese culture.

4. Marine Park: In addition to the land-based attractions, the park also has a Marine Park section. Here, visitors can explore a range of marine and aquatic species through various exhibits and shows. There are opportunities to see dolphins, sea lions, and other marine creatures up close. The park

also offers snorkeling experiences and a water park area for added fun and entertainment.

5. Conservation Efforts: Bali Safari and Marine Park is dedicated to conservation and the protection of endangered species. The park actively supports various conservation programs and initiatives. Visitors can learn about these efforts and the importance of wildlife conservation through educational exhibits and interactive displays.

6. Dining and Shopping: The park offers a range of dining options, from casual cafes to themed restaurants, where visitors can enjoy a meal amidst the natural surroundings. There are also souvenir shops and gift stores where you can find unique items, handicrafts, and memorabilia related to the park and its animal inhabitants.

7. Cultural Experiences: Bali Safari and Marine Park provides opportunities to engage with Balinese culture. Traditional Balinese architecture and design elements are incorporated throughout the park, creating an authentic cultural atmosphere. Visitors can also witness traditional Balinese ceremonies and performances during their visit.

8. Additional Activities: The park offers various additional activities that visitors can enjoy, such as elephant rides, animal feeding sessions, and photo opportunities with certain animals. These activities provide extra moments of excitement and interaction with the park's inhabitants.

When planning a visit to Bali Safari and Marine Park, it's advisable to check the park's website or contact them directly for the most up-to-date information on opening hours, ticket prices, and available experiences.

Sekumpul Waterfall is a stunning natural attraction located in the village of Sekumpul in northern Bali. Here's some information about Sekumpul Waterfall:

1. Location: Sekumpul Waterfall is situated in a lush green valley surrounded by dense forests in the northern part of Bali, near Singaraja. It's about a 2.5 to 3-hour drive from popular tourist areas like Ubud or Seminyak. The waterfall is part of the Sekumpul Village, which is known for its scenic beauty and rice terraces.

2. Majestic Setting: Sekumpul Waterfall is often referred to as one of the most beautiful waterfalls in Bali due to its impressive height and picturesque surroundings. The waterfall is actually a collection of several cascades, with the main waterfall reaching a height of approximately 80 meters (262 feet). The sight of the water rushing down the cliff face into a pool below is truly awe-inspiring.

3. Trekking Adventure: To reach Sekumpul Waterfall, visitors need to embark on a moderate trek through the lush jungle and down a series of steep stairs. The trek involves navigating through narrow paths, crossing streams, and sometimes getting wet. The journey to the waterfall takes about 30-45 minutes, and it's recommended to wear comfortable footwear and bring a bottle of water.

4. Scenic Views: Throughout the trek to Sekumpul Waterfall, you'll be treated to breathtaking views of the surrounding landscape, including terraced rice fields, tropical vegetation, and small villages. The journey itself is an opportunity to immerse yourself in the natural beauty of Bali's countryside.

5. Refreshing Swim: Once you reach the base of Sekumpul Waterfall, you can enjoy a refreshing swim in the natural pool formed

by the cascading water. The cool and clear water offers a welcome respite from the tropical heat. It's advisable to bring a change of clothes if you plan on swimming.

6. Photography Opportunities: Sekumpul Waterfall presents fantastic opportunities for photography enthusiasts. The sheer size and beauty of the waterfall, combined with the lush surroundings, create stunning compositions. It's recommended to bring a waterproof camera or protective gear for your equipment due to the mist and potential water splashes.

7. Local Guides: Hiring a local guide is advisable when visiting Sekumpul Waterfall, especially if it's your first time. They can assist you with navigating the trek, provide information about the area, and ensure your safety. Additionally, they can share local insights and stories about the waterfall and the surrounding community.

8. Conservation and Respect: It's important to practice responsible tourism and respect the natural environment when visiting Sekumpul Waterfall. Avoid littering, stick to designated paths, and follow any instructions or guidelines provided by the local guides or authorities. Respect the local customs and traditions of the area.

Note: Due to the natural terrain and conditions, it's recommended to check the weather and the accessibility of Sekumpul Waterfall before planning your visit. It's also advisable to bring insect repellent, sunscreen, and any necessary personal items for the trek.

Enjoy your visit to Sekumpul Waterfall and take in the breathtaking beauty of this natural wonder in Bali!

The Bali Swing and Tegalalang Rice Terrace Swing are two popular attractions in Bali that offer thrilling swing experiences amidst stunning natural landscapes. Here's some information about these attractions:

1. Bali Swing: The Bali Swing is an adventure park located in the village of Bongkasa, close to Ubud. It offers visitors the opportunity to experience swinging on giant swings suspended high above lush green valleys and tropical forests. The swings vary in height and size, allowing you to choose the one that suits your preference. It's an exhilarating activity that provides panoramic views of the surrounding landscapes.

2. Tegalalang Rice Terrace Swing: Tegalalang Rice Terrace is a famous terraced rice field located in the village of Tegalalang, just north of Ubud. Within the rice terrace area, you can find swing setups that allow you to swing over the picturesque

rice terraces. This swing experience offers a unique perspective of the cascading rice fields and the beauty of Bali's agricultural landscapes.

3. Scenic Views: Both the Bali Swing and the Tegalalang Rice Terrace Swing provide breathtaking views of Bali's natural beauty. From the swings, you can enjoy panoramic vistas of rice terraces, valleys, forests, and distant mountains. It's a great opportunity to capture stunning photographs and immerse yourself in the tranquility of the surroundings.

4. Photography Opportunities: The swings at both locations offer fantastic photo opportunities. The contrasting colors of the rice fields, the lush greenery, and the swing itself create picturesque scenes. Many swings also provide unique photo spots and Instagram-worthy setups, such as bird nests or giant jungle swings.

5. Adrenaline Rush: Swinging on these high-flying swings can be an adrenaline-pumping experience, especially if you're not accustomed to heights. The sensation of soaring through the air above the landscapes adds an extra element of excitement and adventure to your visit.

6. Additional Activities: In addition to the swings, both locations often offer additional activities and attractions. These can include zip lines, photo booths, bird-watching, jungle trekking, and various photo spots. You can spend some time exploring the area, enjoying local cuisine at nearby restaurants, or shopping for souvenirs at the on-site stores.

7. Safety and Precautions: Before participating in the swing experiences, make sure to adhere to the safety guidelines provided by the operators. They typically require guests to wear safety equipment such as harnesses and helmets. It's

important to follow these guidelines to ensure a safe and enjoyable experience.

8. Entrance Fees and Packages: The swing experiences at the Bali Swing and Tegalalang Rice Terrace Swing usually require an entrance fee. They may offer different packages that include various swing options, additional activities, and access to photo spots. It's advisable to check the official websites or contact the operators in advance to get accurate information about pricing and available packages.

Note: As with any tourist attraction, it's recommended to visit during weekdays or non-peak hours to avoid large crowds and long queues.

Enjoy the thrilling swing experiences and the stunning views of Bali's landscapes at the Bali Swing and Tegalalang Rice Terrace Swing!

The official website for the Bali Swing and Tegalalang Rice Terrace Swing is **https://baliswing.com/**. You can book your tickets online or by phone. The cost of a ticket is 200,000 IDR (about $13.70) for adults and 100,000 IDR (about $6.85) for children.

Here are the steps on how to book your tickets online:

1. Go to the Bali Swing website.
2. Click on the "Book Now" button.
3. Choose the date and time of your visit.
4. Enter your personal information.
5. Pay for your tickets.

You will receive a confirmation email with your ticket information.

Here are the steps on how to book your tickets by phone:

1. Call the Bali Swing office at +62 361 975 7575.
2. Choose the date and time of your visit.
3. Provide your personal information.
4. Pay for your tickets.

You will receive a confirmation call with your ticket information.

Here are some tips for visiting the Bali Swing and Tegalalang Rice Terrace Swing:

* Wear comfortable shoes. You will be doing a lot of walking around the rice terraces.
* Bring a camera. You will want to capture all of the amazing views.
* Be prepared for crowds. The Bali Swing is a popular tourist destination, so expect to be sharing the space with other people.
* Be respectful of the locals. The Balinese are very friendly and welcoming, so be sure to be respectful of their culture and traditions.

Traditional Balinese Dishes to Try

When indulging in Balinese cuisine, you'll have the opportunity to savor a variety of flavorful dishes that reflect the unique culinary heritage of the Indonesian island of Bali. Here are some traditional Balinese dishes you should try:

1. Babi Guling: This is Bali's most famous dish, a whole roasted suckling pig. The pig is seasoned with a blend of spices, including turmeric, coriander, lemongrass, and garlic, then slowly roasted to perfection. Babi Guling is typically served with rice, lawar (a mix of vegetables, coconut, and spices), and crispy crackling.

2. Ayam Betutu: Another popular Balinese specialty, Ayam Betutu is a whole chicken

stuffed with a spice paste made from shallots, garlic, chili, ginger, turmeric, and other aromatic ingredients. The chicken is then wrapped in banana leaves and slow-cooked, resulting in tender and flavorful meat.

3. Bebek Betutu: Similar to Ayam Betutu, Bebek Betutu is a dish made with duck instead of chicken. It follows a similar preparation process and is equally delicious, with the rich flavors of the spice paste permeating the tender duck meat.

4. Lawar: Lawar is a traditional Balinese salad that consists of finely chopped green beans, coconut, shallots, garlic, and a mix of spices. It's usually served with rice and often accompanies dishes like Babi Guling or Ayam Betutu.

5. Sate Lilit: These flavorful Balinese satays are made from minced meat (usually chicken, pork, or fish) mixed with a variety of

spices, grated coconut, and herbs. The mixture is then wrapped around a lemongrass skewer and grilled over hot charcoal.

6. Nasi Campur: Nasi Campur translates to "mixed rice" and is a popular dish that combines steamed rice with an assortment of small portions of various Balinese dishes, such as fried chicken, grilled fish, sambal (chili sauce), vegetables, and spicy tempeh.

7. Sambal Matah: This traditional Balinese condiment is made from a mix of finely chopped shallots, lemongrass, chili peppers, lime juice, and shrimp paste. It adds a fiery and tangy kick to any dish and is particularly delicious when paired with grilled meats or fish.

8. Bubur Mengguh: This Balinese rice porridge is a comforting dish made by simmering rice with coconut milk and spices like pandan leaves and ginger. It is often

served as a breakfast or dessert option and can be topped with sliced fruits or sweet coconut.

These are just a few examples of the delicious traditional Balinese dishes you can explore. Balinese cuisine offers a rich tapestry of flavors, blending spices, fresh ingredients, and cultural influences to create a truly unique dining experience.

Popular Local Food Markets and Warungs

When it comes to experiencing the vibrant food culture of Bali, exploring the local food markets and warungs (small food stalls or eateries) is a must. Here are some popular food markets and warungs in Bali:

1. Ubud Market: Located in the heart of Ubud, this bustling market offers a wide

array of fresh produce, spices, and traditional Balinese snacks. You can also find handicrafts, clothing, and souvenirs here. After exploring the market, head to the nearby warungs to enjoy local specialties.

2. Gianyar Night Market: Situated in Gianyar town, this night market comes alive after sunset. It's a great place to sample authentic Balinese street food at affordable prices. From satay to grilled seafood, mie goreng (fried noodles), and traditional sweets, you'll find a variety of tasty treats to satisfy your cravings.

3. Sanur Night Market: Located in the coastal town of Sanur, this bustling night market is a favorite among locals and tourists alike. You can find a wide range of local dishes such as babi guling, sate, nasi campur, and fresh seafood. The market also offers a lively atmosphere and a chance to mingle with the locals.

4. Kuta Art Market: Situated near Kuta Beach, this market is known for its handicrafts, artwork, and souvenirs. While exploring the stalls, you'll also find local food vendors offering dishes like nasi goreng (fried rice), grilled chicken, and refreshing coconut water.

5. Pasar Badung: Located in Denpasar, the capital of Bali, Pasar Badung is the largest traditional market on the island. It's a bustling hub of activity with vendors selling a wide variety of fresh fruits, vegetables, spices, and local snacks. You can also find cooked food stalls offering traditional Balinese dishes.

6. Warung Made: This iconic warung in Seminyak has been serving Balinese cuisine for decades. It offers a cozy ambiance and a menu featuring classic dishes like nasi campur, grilled satays, and bebek betutu. Warung Made is a popular

spot for both locals and tourists looking for an authentic dining experience.

7. Warung Babi Guling Ibu Oka: Located in Ubud, this warung is renowned for its signature dish, babi guling. It serves succulent roasted suckling pig with crispy skin, accompanied by flavorful sides such as lawar and sambal matah.

8. Warung Sopa: Situated in Sanur, Warung Sopa is a vegetarian-friendly eatery that focuses on fresh and healthy Balinese cuisine. They offer a variety of vegetarian and vegan options, including nasi campur, tempeh dishes, and refreshing juices.

These are just a few examples of the popular food markets and warungs in Bali. Exploring these places will give you a chance to savor authentic Balinese flavors and interact with the locals while immersing yourself in the island's vibrant food culture.

Upscale Dining Experiences

If you're looking for upscale dining experiences in Bali, the island offers a range of exquisite restaurants that combine delectable cuisine with stunning settings. Here are some upscale dining options to consider:

1. Locavore: Located in Ubud, Locavore is a renowned restaurant that focuses on using locally sourced ingredients to create innovative dishes. The menu showcases a blend of Indonesian flavors with international culinary techniques. Locavore offers both a tasting menu and à la carte options.

2. Mozaic: Situated in Ubud, Mozaic is a fine-dining establishment that offers a unique culinary journey. The restaurant presents a gourmet fusion of Indonesian and French cuisine, using premium ingredients and innovative cooking

methods. The tasting menus at Mozaic are meticulously crafted to provide an exceptional dining experience.

3. Swept Away at The Samaya: Nestled along the Ayung River in Ubud, Swept Away offers an intimate and romantic setting for a special dining experience. You can dine on a floating deck surrounded by lush greenery while enjoying a menu that highlights fresh seafood, grilled meats, and flavorful Balinese-inspired dishes.

4. Kayuputi at The St. Regis Bali Resort: Located in Nusa Dua, Kayuputi is an elegant beachfront restaurant known for its refined atmosphere and gourmet cuisine. The menu features a mix of Asian and international flavors, with a focus on seafood. The restaurant offers an extensive wine list to complement the dining experience.

5. Ju-Ma-Na at Banyan Tree Ungasan: Perched on a cliff in Uluwatu, Ju-Ma-Na offers breathtaking views of the Indian Ocean. The restaurant specializes in contemporary French cuisine with Japanese influences. Guests can enjoy a sophisticated dining experience while taking in the panoramic vistas.

6. Sundara at Four Seasons Resort Bali at Jimbaran Bay: Sundara offers a luxurious beachfront dining experience in Jimbaran. The restaurant serves a diverse range of dishes, including international favorites and Balinese specialties. Sundara is known for its stylish ambiance, stunning sunset views, and live music.

7. Merah Putih: Located in Seminyak, Merah Putih combines modern design with traditional Indonesian flavors. The restaurant offers an upscale dining experience in a beautifully designed space. The menu showcases a mix of regional

Indonesian dishes using high-quality ingredients.

8. Kubu at Mandapa, a Ritz-Carlton Reserve: Situated in Ubud, Kubu offers an enchanting dining experience within bamboo structures overlooking the Ayung River. The restaurant specializes in Mediterranean-European cuisine with an emphasis on seafood. The elegant setting and tranquil ambiance add to the allure of the dining experience.

These upscale dining experiences in Bali provide an opportunity to indulge in exceptional culinary creations while immersing yourself in the island's enchanting surroundings and luxurious hospitality. It's advisable to make reservations in advance, especially during peak seasons, to secure your preferred dining experience.

Vegetarian and Vegan Options

Bali has a growing number of vegetarian and vegan options, making it a great destination for those with plant-based dietary preferences. Here are some restaurants and eateries in Bali that cater to vegetarian and vegan diets:

1. Earth Café: With multiple locations in Ubud, Seminyak, and Tampaksiring, Earth Café offers a diverse menu of vegetarian, vegan, and raw food options. They serve everything from salads and wraps to burgers, pizzas, and desserts, using organic and locally sourced ingredients.

2. The Seeds of Life: Located in Ubud, The Seeds of Life specializes in raw, vegan, and vegetarian cuisine. Their menu features a variety of raw food dishes, smoothies,

juices, and desserts. They also offer raw food workshops and classes.

3. Zula Vegetarian Paradise: Situated in Seminyak, Zula Vegetarian Paradise is a popular spot for vegetarian and vegan dining. They serve a mix of international and Indonesian-inspired dishes, including falafel, curries, wraps, and smoothies.

4. Soma Café: Located in Ubud, Soma Café is a vegan and vegetarian restaurant known for its wholesome and nutritious offerings. They offer a variety of plant-based dishes, including salads, bowls, wraps, and raw food options.

5. Alchemy: Situated in Ubud, Alchemy is a well-known vegetarian and vegan café and health food store. They serve a wide range of salads, wraps, raw desserts, and juices. Alchemy also offers a salad bar where you can create your own customized salad.

6. Clear Café: With locations in Ubud and Canggu, Clear Café offers a diverse menu with vegetarian, vegan, and gluten-free options. They focus on using organic and locally sourced ingredients to create flavorful dishes, including salads, stir-fries, burgers, and smoothies.

7. Moksa Plant-based Cuisine & Permaculture: Located in Ubud, Moksa is a vegan restaurant that showcases organic, plant-based cuisine. They have an on-site permaculture garden and offer a farm-to-table dining experience. Moksa serves creative dishes like jackfruit tacos, tempeh burgers, and raw food desserts.

8. Sage Bali: Situated in Ubud, Sage Bali is a vegan restaurant that offers a range of dishes made with organic and locally sourced ingredients. Their menu includes salads, soups, sandwiches, and main courses, with gluten-free options available.

These are just a few examples of the vegetarian and vegan dining options in Bali. Additionally, many restaurants across the island offer vegetarian and vegan choices or can accommodate dietary requests with prior notice. It's always recommended to inform the staff about your dietary preferences to ensure a satisfying dining experience.

Surfing and Beaches

Bali, Indonesia, is renowned for its beautiful beaches and world-class surfing spots. Whether you're a seasoned surfer or a beginner looking to catch your first wave, Bali offers a wide range of beaches and surf breaks to suit all skill levels. Here are some popular surfing destinations and beaches in Bali:

1. Kuta Beach: Located in the heart of Bali's tourist hub, Kuta Beach is a popular spot for beginners due to its consistent waves and

surf schools offering lessons. It can get crowded, especially during peak season, but it's a great place to learn and practice.

2. Uluwatu: Uluwatu is home to some of Bali's most famous surf breaks. It's known for its powerful waves and long rides, making it a favorite among experienced surfers. Uluwatu is also home to the iconic Uluwatu Temple perched on a cliff, offering stunning views of the surf below.

3. Padang Padang: Located near Uluwatu, Padang Padang is a beautiful white sand beach with a reef break that produces consistent left-hand barrels. It's a challenging wave suitable for intermediate to advanced surfers. The beach's natural beauty makes it a popular spot for both surfers and sunbathers.

4. Canggu: Canggu has become one of Bali's trendiest surf spots, offering a variety of breaks for all levels. Berawa Beach, Batu

Bolong Beach, and Echo Beach are the main surf breaks in Canggu. It's a vibrant area with a great surf culture, numerous cafes, and a thriving nightlife scene.

5. Medewi: Located on Bali's west coast, Medewi is known for its long left-hand point break. It's a mellow and forgiving wave, perfect for beginners and longboarders. Medewi offers a more relaxed and less crowded surfing experience compared to some of the other popular spots in Bali.

6. Nusa Lembongan and Nusa Ceningan: These neighboring islands off the southeast coast of Bali are known for their stunning beaches and great surf breaks. Playgrounds, Lacerations, and Shipwrecks are some of the surf breaks you can find in this area. The waves here are generally more challenging, attracting experienced surfers.

7. Serangan: Located just a short drive from the popular tourist areas, Serangan is a hidden gem with consistent reef breaks. It's suitable for both intermediate and advanced surfers, offering left and right-hand waves. Serangan is often less crowded, providing a more relaxed surfing experience.

Remember to check the surf conditions, tides, and local regulations before heading out to any surf spot. It's also a good idea to respect the environment and local customs while enjoying Bali's beautiful beaches and surf breaks.

Scuba Diving and Snorkeling

Bali is not only a paradise for surfers but also offers incredible opportunities for scuba diving and snorkeling. With its diverse marine life, vibrant coral reefs, and clear waters, Bali attracts divers and snorkelers from around the world. Here are some popular scuba diving and snorkeling spots in Bali:

1. Tulamben: Located on the northeast coast of Bali, Tulamben is famous for the USAT Liberty shipwreck. This World War II wreck lies close to the shore and has become an artificial reef, attracting a wide variety of marine life. Tulamben offers excellent diving and snorkeling opportunities with calm conditions and great visibility.

2. Nusa Penida and Nusa Lembongan: These neighboring islands off Bali's southeast coast are known for their stunning underwater landscapes. Crystal Bay, Manta Point, and Blue Corner are popular dive sites around Nusa Penida and Nusa Lembongan. Here, you can encounter manta rays, colorful coral reefs, and the

chance to spot the magnificent Mola Mola (sunfish) during the right season.

3. Menjangan Island: Located in the northwest part of Bali, Menjangan Island is part of the West Bali National Park. This protected area offers pristine coral reefs, crystal-clear waters, and an abundance of marine life. Divers and snorkelers can explore vibrant coral gardens, encounter schools of tropical fish, and even spot reef sharks and sea turtles.

4. Amed: Amed is a small coastal village on Bali's northeast coast and is known for its relaxed atmosphere and diverse underwater scenery. The area features a mix of coral reefs, walls, and shipwrecks, providing various dive sites suitable for different skill levels. The underwater landscape here is teeming with colorful marine life, making it a great spot for both diving and snorkeling.

5. Padang Bai: Located on Bali's east coast, Padang Bai offers a range of dive sites suitable for all levels. Blue Lagoon and Bias Tugel are popular spots for snorkeling, featuring clear waters, vibrant corals, and a wide variety of fish species. The nearby dive sites of Padang Bai, such as the Jepun and Tanjung Sari reefs, offer opportunities to explore deeper waters and encounter larger marine species.

6. Secret Bay: Located in the northwestern part of Bali near Gilimanuk, Secret Bay is a unique diving spot known for its rich macro marine life. Divers can discover rare critters like seahorses, frogfish, and ghost pipefish in the black volcanic sands of this area. It's a paradise for macro photography enthusiasts and those interested in the smaller, hidden treasures of the ocean.

When engaging in scuba diving or snorkeling, it's important to prioritize safety and follow responsible diving practices.

Ensure you have the necessary certifications, dive with reputable operators, and respect the marine environment by not touching or damaging the coral reefs or marine life.

White Water Rafting

Bali offers thrilling white water rafting experiences for adventure enthusiasts. The island's rivers provide opportunities for exciting rafting adventures amidst stunning natural landscapes. Here are some popular white water rafting destinations in Bali:

1. Ayung River: Located in central Bali, the Ayung River is the most popular white water rafting spot on the island. Rafting down the Ayung River allows you to immerse yourself in Bali's lush rainforest, passing by stunning waterfalls, rice terraces, and tropical scenery. The rapids range from class II to

class III, making it suitable for beginners and those seeking a fun and scenic rafting experience.

2. Telaga Waja River: Situated in East Bali, the Telaga Waja River offers an exhilarating white water rafting adventure. This river boasts more challenging rapids, ranging from class III to class IV, making it ideal for thrill-seekers and those with previous rafting experience. Rafting on the Telaga Waja River also offers breathtaking views of rice paddies, valleys, and cliffs.

3. Melangit River: Located in Klungkung, the Melangit River is a lesser-known rafting spot, perfect for those seeking a more secluded and off-the-beaten-path experience. The rapids here range from class II to class IV, providing an exciting rafting journey through scenic gorges and tropical surroundings.

4. Pakerisan River: The Pakerisan River is situated in Gianyar, east of Ubud, and offers a tranquil and scenic rafting experience. The rapids on the Pakerisan River are relatively calm, ranging from class I to class II, making it suitable for families and beginners. Rafting on this river allows you to explore the lush green landscapes and traditional Balinese villages.

When participating in white water rafting, it's important to choose a reputable rafting operator that prioritizes safety and provides professional guides. They will provide you with safety equipment, including life jackets and helmets, and give instructions on rafting techniques. It's also advisable to wear appropriate clothing, such as quick-drying shorts and a t-shirt, and bring a change of clothes for after the rafting trip.

White water rafting in Bali is a thrilling adventure that combines adrenaline-pumping rapids with breathtaking natural scenery, offering an unforgettable experience for adventure enthusiasts visiting the island.

Mountaineering and Hiking Trails

Bali, an Indonesian island known for its stunning beaches and vibrant culture, also offers some excellent opportunities for mountaineering and hiking. While it may not have towering peaks like other mountainous regions, Bali still boasts several scenic trails and volcanoes that provide rewarding outdoor experiences. Here are some notable mountaineering and hiking trails in Bali:

1. Mount Batur: Located in the northeast part of Bali, Mount Batur is an active volcano that offers a popular hiking experience. The trek usually starts early in the morning to reach the summit in time for a breathtaking sunrise. It takes about two to three hours to ascend to the top, and the trail is well-marked. The panoramic views of

Lake Batur and the surrounding landscapes make it a worthwhile climb.

2. Mount Agung: As Bali's highest peak, Mount Agung stands at 3,031 meters (9,944 feet). This challenging climb attracts experienced mountaineers seeking an adventure. The ascent requires physical fitness and stamina, as well as proper equipment. It usually takes around six to eight hours to reach the summit. However, due to the volcanic activity, it's essential to check with local authorities regarding the current status and any restrictions.

3. Campuhan Ridge Walk: For those looking for a more relaxed and scenic hiking experience, the Campuhan Ridge Walk in Ubud is an excellent choice. This trail takes you through lush green hills, rice fields, and small villages. The walk typically starts at the Campuhan Bridge and stretches for about 2 kilometers (1.2 miles). It offers

picturesque views and is ideal for capturing stunning photos of Bali's countryside.

4. Sekumpul Waterfall Trek: Located in the northern region of Bali, the Sekumpul Waterfall is one of the island's most impressive natural wonders. To reach the waterfall, you'll embark on a moderately challenging trek through forests, across rivers, and down steep paths. The journey can be physically demanding, but the reward of witnessing the magnificent cascade of water makes it worth it.

5. Mount Batukaru: Situated in Bali's central region, Mount Batukaru is a dormant volcano surrounded by lush rainforests. The trek to the summit is a peaceful and serene experience, taking you through dense vegetation and ancient temples. It is less crowded compared to other trails, providing a tranquil atmosphere for hikers who seek solitude.

Please note that when embarking on any mountaineering or hiking adventure, it's crucial to prioritize safety and be adequately prepared. Consider hiring a local guide, wearing appropriate gear, carrying sufficient water and snacks, and checking the weather conditions beforehand. Additionally, respecting the environment and local customs is essential to preserve the natural beauty of these trails.

Yoga and Wellness Retreats

Bali is renowned as a popular destination for yoga and wellness retreats, offering a serene and spiritual environment that attracts people from around the world. Whether you're a beginner or an experienced yogi, there are numerous retreats and centers throughout the island that cater to different preferences and levels of practice. Here are some notable yoga and wellness retreats in Bali:

1. The Yoga Barn (Ubud): Located in the cultural heart of Bali, Ubud, The Yoga Barn is one of the most well-known yoga centers on the island. It offers a wide range of classes, workshops, and retreats led by experienced instructors from various yoga traditions. The Yoga Barn also provides a serene environment with lush surroundings and dedicated spaces for meditation and healing.

2. Fivelements Retreat Bali (Mambal): Fivelements Retreat Bali is a luxury wellness retreat nestled in the outskirts of Ubud. This eco-conscious retreat focuses on holistic healing and offers a range of wellness programs that combine yoga, meditation, spa treatments, and healthy cuisine. The serene setting by the Ayung River creates a peaceful ambiance for relaxation and rejuvenation.

3. Soulshine Bali (Ubud): Owned by musician and philanthropist Michael Franti, Soulshine Bali is a boutique hotel and yoga retreat center. It offers daily yoga classes, workshops, and personalized retreats with experienced instructors. With beautiful accommodations and lush gardens, Soulshine Bali provides a tranquil and inspiring setting for a wellness getaway.

4. COMO Shambhala Estate (Payangan): Situated amidst the lush tropical rainforest near Ubud, COMO Shambhala Estate is a luxury wellness retreat known for its holistic approach to wellbeing. The retreat offers yoga and meditation classes, wellness consultations, spa treatments, and specialized wellness programs. The serene atmosphere, nutritious cuisine, and luxurious accommodations make it a haven for relaxation and self-discovery.

5. Blooming Lotus Yoga (Lodtunduh): Blooming Lotus Yoga is a yoga retreat center that focuses on traditional yoga practices and spiritual growth. Located in a peaceful village outside Ubud, it offers immersive retreats and teacher training programs. The retreats include daily yoga classes, meditation sessions, workshops, and cultural excursions, providing a well-rounded experience of Balinese culture and spirituality.

These are just a few examples of the many yoga and wellness retreats available in Bali. It's advisable to research and choose a retreat that aligns with your interests, preferences, and level of experience. Whether you seek relaxation, self-reflection, or a deeper spiritual connection, Bali's yoga and wellness retreats offer an opportunity to nourish your mind, body, and soul in a beautiful and tranquil setting.

Traditional Balinese arts and crafts

are an integral part of Balinese culture and have a rich history dating back centuries. Balinese artisans are known for their skillful craftsmanship and attention to detail, creating beautiful and intricate artworks using various materials and techniques. Here are some examples of traditional Balinese arts and crafts:

1. Woodcarving: Woodcarving is a prominent art form in Bali. Skilled artisans carve intricate designs, often depicting mythological figures, deities, or scenes from Hindu epics, into various types of wood. Woodcarvings can be found in the form of statues, masks, architectural elements, furniture, and decorative objects.

2. Silver and Gold Jewelry: Balinese artisans are renowned for their exquisite silver and gold jewelry. They use traditional techniques such as filigree and granulation

to create intricate designs featuring motifs inspired by nature, Balinese mythology, and Hindu symbolism. Traditional jewelry pieces include rings, bracelets, necklaces, earrings, and ceremonial accessories.

3. Batik: Batik is a traditional textile art form in Bali, where artisans use wax-resistant dyeing techniques to create intricate patterns on fabric. The process involves applying melted wax to the cloth, which acts as a barrier to the dye. The fabric is then dyed, and the wax is removed to reveal the desired pattern. Batik fabrics are used to make clothing, scarves, wall hangings, and other decorative items.

4. Painting: Balinese painting is characterized by vibrant colors, intricate details, and themes inspired by mythology and religious stories. Traditional Balinese paintings often depict scenes from Hindu epics such as the Ramayana and the Mahabharata. Artists use a variety of

mediums, including ink, watercolor, and natural pigments made from minerals and plant materials.

5. Gamelan Instruments: Gamelan is a traditional ensemble music of Bali, consisting of various percussion instruments such as metallophones, xylophones, drums, and gongs. Balinese artisans handcraft these instruments, meticulously tuning each piece to create harmonious sounds. The instruments are often adorned with intricate carvings and decorative elements.

6. Stone Carving: Balinese stone carving is another significant art form, commonly seen in temples, palaces, and public buildings. Artisans sculpt intricate statues, reliefs, and decorative elements from volcanic rock or coral stone. These carvings often depict deities, mythological creatures, and scenes from Hindu epics.

7. Mask Making: Masks play a vital role in Balinese rituals and performances. Artisans create traditional masks, typically made from wood, and hand-paint them with vibrant colors. These masks are used in dance dramas, such as the Barong dance, to represent various characters and spirits.

These are just a few examples of the traditional arts and crafts of Bali. Balinese artisans continue to preserve and innovate these ancient techniques, contributing to the cultural richness and artistic heritage of the island.

Balinese temples and rituals hold great significance in the religious and cultural life of the Balinese people. Hinduism, specifically a unique form known as Balinese Hinduism, is the predominant religion practiced in Bali. Here's an overview of Balinese temples and some of the rituals associated with them:

1. Pura (Temple): Bali is dotted with numerous puras, which are Hindu temples found in various sizes and designs. Each village in Bali typically has at least three main temples: the Pura Puseh (temple of origin), the Pura Desa (village temple), and the Pura Dalem (temple of the dead). These temples serve as spiritual and communal centers for the local communities.

2. Temple Architecture: Balinese temple architecture is characterized by its intricacy and unique design elements. Temples are often built on elevated ground and feature multi-tiered meru towers, split gates (called candi bentar), and stone carvings depicting mythological figures and scenes. The architecture is designed to represent the Hindu cosmology and symbolize the connection between humans, gods, and the universe.

3. Odalan: Odalan refers to the temple anniversary celebration, which is held every 210 days based on the Balinese calendar system. During the Odalan, the temple is adorned with decorations, offerings are made, and religious ceremonies take place. The celebrations involve traditional music, dance performances, and processions. It is a time when the local community gathers to pay homage to the temple deities and seek their blessings.

4. Melasti: Melasti is a purification ritual that takes place before Nyepi, the Balinese New Year. It involves a procession to the nearest water source, such as the beach or river, where devotees cleanse themselves and sacred objects, such as temple heirlooms and sacred statues. Melasti is seen as a way to purify and rejuvenate the spiritual energy of the village and its inhabitants.

5. Galungan and Kuningan: Galungan is a major Balinese Hindu festival that

celebrates the victory of dharma (good) over adharma (evil). It occurs every 210 days and lasts for ten days. During Galungan, families erect tall bamboo poles called "penjor" outside their homes, and temples are beautifully adorned. Offerings are made to ancestors and deities, and various rituals and ceremonies take place. Kuningan marks the end of the Galungan period with special offerings and prayers.

6. Ngaben: Ngaben, also known as the cremation ceremony, is a significant ritual in Balinese Hinduism. It is believed that through cremation, the soul can be released from the body and reach the afterlife. Ngaben ceremonies can be elaborate and involve a procession, traditional music, and a large-scale cremation pyre. They are seen as an important duty to honor the deceased and ensure a proper spiritual journey.

7. Saraswati: Saraswati is a festival dedicated to the goddess of knowledge,

arts, and learning. It is celebrated every six months to invoke blessings for wisdom and intellect. On Saraswati day, Balinese Hindus offer prayers, make offerings, and engage in activities related to education, such as reading books and visiting libraries.

These are just a few examples of the temples and rituals in Balinese Hinduism. The religious practices and ceremonies vary across different regions and communities in Bali, but they all play a vital role in upholding the spiritual and cultural fabric of the island.

Balinese dance and music

are highly expressive and dynamic art forms that play a central role in Balinese culture. They are deeply intertwined with religious ceremonies, cultural events, and storytelling traditions. Here's an overview of Balinese dance and music:

Balinese Dance:

1. Barong Dance: The Barong dance is one of the most famous and beloved dances in Bali. It tells the story of the eternal battle between good (Barong) and evil (Rangda). Performers wear elaborate costumes, including the Barong, a mythical creature, and dancers depict various characters, engaging in dramatic movements and choreography.

2. Legong Dance: Legong is a classical dance performed by young girls. It is characterized by intricate finger movements, precise footwork, and expressive facial expressions. Legong dancers often wear ornate costumes and perform to traditional Gamelan music. The dance usually tells a romantic or mythical story.

3. Kecak Dance: The Kecak dance is a unique and mesmerising performance where a large group of male dancers sits in a circle, chanting "cak" rhythmically. The

dance typically depicts scenes from the Hindu epic, Ramayana, and dancers reenact the adventures of Prince Rama. The synchronised chanting creates a trance-like atmosphere.

4. Baris Dance: Baris is a warrior dance that showcases the strength, agility, and masculine prowess of the performer. Dancers imitate the movements of a warrior, wielding a Kris (traditional dagger) or a spear. The dance is accompanied by the powerful beats of Gamelan instruments.

5. Topeng Dance: Topeng is a mask dance that portrays various characters from Balinese folklore and mythology. Performers wear masks representing gods, heroes, or comedic figures and convey their stories through stylized movements and gestures. Topeng dances are often comedic or moralistic in nature.

Balinese Music:

1. Gamelan: Gamelan is the traditional ensemble music of Bali, consisting of a variety of percussion instruments such as metallophones, xylophones, drums, gongs, and bamboo flutes. The ensemble creates complex and rhythmic melodies that accompany dance performances, rituals, and ceremonies. Gamelan music is known for its layered, interlocking patterns and intricate interplay between different instruments.

2. Gender Wayang: Gender Wayang is a traditional Balinese music ensemble consisting of a set of tuned metallophones. The musicians play melodic patterns, often in a call-and-response style, using mallets. Gender Wayang is typically performed in temple ceremonies and shadow puppet shows (wayang kulit).

3. Jegog: Jegog is a unique form of Balinese bamboo music originating from the island's western region. It uses large

bamboo instruments, known as jegog, which produce deep, resonant sounds. The ensemble creates powerful and rhythmic music, often accompanied by dynamic dance performances.

4. Angklung: Angklung is a traditional bamboo musical instrument found in Bali and other parts of Indonesia. It consists of several bamboo tubes attached to a frame, and each tube produces a different pitch when shaken. Angklung ensembles create melodious tunes and are often used in communal music-making.

These are just a few examples of Balinese dance and music forms. They reflect the creativity, spirituality, and vibrant cultural traditions of the Balinese people, captivating audiences with their beauty, grace, and expressive storytelling.

Festivals and Celebrations

Bali is known for its vibrant and colourful festivals and celebrations, which are deeply rooted in its rich cultural and religious heritage. These festivities provide a glimpse into the island's traditions, customs, and community spirit. Here are some of the notable festivals and celebrations in Bali:

1. Nyepi (Day of Silence): Nyepi is the Balinese New Year celebration and is considered the most important cultural event on the island. It is a day of complete silence, fasting, and self-reflection. Balinese Hindus observe Nyepi by staying indoors, refraining from work and entertainment, and keeping lights turned off. The purpose is to cleanse and purify the island of negative influences, followed by the festive days of Ogoh-Ogoh and Ngrupuk the night before and after Nyepi.

2. Galungan and Kuningan: Galungan is a major Balinese Hindu festival that celebrates the victory of dharma (good) over adharma (evil). It occurs every 210 days and lasts for ten days. Balinese families erect tall bamboo poles called "penjor" outside their homes, and temples are beautifully adorned. Offerings are made to ancestors and deities, and various rituals and ceremonies take place. Kuningan marks the end of the Galungan period with special offerings and prayers.

3. Saraswati: Saraswati is a festival dedicated to the goddess of knowledge, arts, and learning. It is celebrated every six months to invoke blessings for wisdom and intellect. On Saraswati day, Balinese Hindus offer prayers, make offerings, and engage in activities related to education, such as reading books and visiting libraries.

4. Pagerwesi: Pagerwesi is a festival that commemorates the dedication of the mind

and spiritual protection. It is held four days after Saraswati day. Balinese Hindus pray for strength and protection against negative forces during this festival. Special ceremonies are conducted at temples, and offerings are made to deities.

5. Tumpek: Tumpek is a series of festivals dedicated to various aspects of Balinese life. Tumpek Landep celebrates metal objects, Tumpek Uduh honours plants and agriculture, Tumpek Kandang focuses on animals and livestock, and Tumpek Krulut is dedicated to musical instruments. These festivals involve prayers, blessings, and offerings to show gratitude and seek blessings for each specific aspect.

6. Piodalan (Temple Anniversaries): Piodalan refers to the anniversary celebrations of Balinese temples. Each temple has its own unique celebration, typically held once a year based on the temple's specific calendar date. Piodalan

involves special rituals, prayers, processions, traditional music and dance performances, and offerings to honour the temple deities.

7. Ubud Writers and Readers Festival: While not strictly religious, the Ubud Writers and Readers Festival is a renowned cultural event that attracts international and local writers, intellectuals, and artists. It celebrates literature, art, and ideas through panel discussions, book launches, performances, workshops, and other activities. The festival promotes dialogue, creativity, and cross-cultural exchange.

These are just a few examples of the diverse festivals and celebrations that take place in Bali throughout the year. They showcase the island's cultural vibrancy, spiritual devotion, and community cohesion, creating a tapestry of experiences for locals and visitors alike.

Shopping and Souvenirs

Ubud Art Market

The Ubud Art Market is a popular shopping destination located in the town of Ubud in Bali, Indonesia. It is known for its vibrant and diverse collection of traditional Balinese arts and crafts. Here's some information about the Ubud Art Market and what you can expect when shopping there:

Location: The Ubud Art Market is situated in the central part of Ubud, near the Ubud Palace (Puri Saren Ubud). It is easily accessible and within walking distance from many hotels and accommodations in the area.

Merchandise: The market offers a wide range of traditional Balinese goods, including intricate woodcarvings, paintings, batik and ikat textiles, silver jewelry, traditional masks, handmade woven bags, sarongs, and various other handicrafts. You'll also find items such as dreamcatchers, traditional musical instruments, home decor items, and souvenirs.

Authenticity: While there are some mass-produced items available, you can also find many unique and authentic pieces created by local artisans. Take your time to explore the market, as different vendors offer varying styles, quality, and prices. Bargaining is common in this market, so feel free to negotiate the price with the sellers.

Tips for Shopping:
1. Compare prices: Since there are multiple stalls selling similar items, it's a good idea to compare prices before making a purchase. This will help you get an idea of the average price range and allow you to negotiate better.

2. Quality check: Examine the items closely for quality. If you're purchasing artwork, look for good brushwork, detailing, and vibrant colors. When buying textiles, check the fabric quality, stitching, and patterns.

3. Be respectful: The sellers at the Ubud Art Market are generally friendly, so it's important to be polite and respectful during your interactions. Remember that bargaining is a common practice, but do so in a friendly manner.

4. Cash is king: Most vendors in the market prefer cash transactions, so it's advisable to carry enough Indonesian Rupiah (IDR). There are also ATMs available nearby if you need to withdraw cash.

5. Opening hours: The Ubud Art Market is usually open from early morning until late afternoon. However, it's always a good idea to check the specific opening hours during your visit, as they may vary.

Overall, the Ubud Art Market offers a delightful shopping experience where you can find unique traditional Balinese crafts and souvenirs. Enjoy exploring the market and discovering the rich cultural heritage of Bali!

The Seminyak shopping district
 is another popular shopping destination in Bali, located in the Seminyak area, which is known for its trendy and upscale atmosphere. Here's some information about the Seminyak shopping district and what you can expect when shopping there:

Location: The Seminyak shopping district is situated along Jalan Raya Seminyak, the main road that runs through the area. It is easily accessible and located not far from popular tourist areas like Kuta and Legian.

Merchandise: The shopping district offers a mix of local boutiques, designer stores, art galleries, homeware shops, and concept stores. You can find a wide range of items including fashion clothing, accessories, beachwear, jewelry, leather goods, artwork, home decor, and unique souvenirs. Many of the products cater to the trendy and fashionable crowd.

International and Local Brands: In Seminyak, you'll find a mix of international brands and local designers. Some well-known international brands have their flagship stores in Seminyak, alongside a variety of local boutiques showcasing the work of talented Indonesian designers.

Concept Stores and Lifestyle Boutiques: Seminyak is known for its concept stores and lifestyle boutiques that offer a curated selection of fashion, homeware, and unique products. These stores often feature a blend of local and international brands and provide a more personalized shopping experience.

Art Galleries: If you're interested in art, Seminyak is home to several art galleries where you can find contemporary and traditional Balinese artwork. These galleries showcase a range of mediums, including paintings, sculptures, and mixed media pieces.

Cafes and Restaurants: The shopping district in Seminyak is also dotted with trendy cafes and restaurants, providing plenty of opportunities for a coffee break or a delicious meal while you explore the area.

Opening Hours: Most shops in Seminyak open around 10:00 AM and close around 9:00 PM. However, some stores may have slightly different operating hours, so it's a good idea to check before visiting.

Seminyak offers a more upscale and cosmopolitan shopping experience compared to other areas in Bali. It's a great place to find unique fashion pieces, designer items, and stylish souvenirs. Enjoy exploring the Seminyak shopping district and indulge in some retail therapy during your visit to Bali!

Traditional Handicrafts and Artwork
When it comes to traditional handicrafts and artwork in Bali, there are several iconic items that showcase the rich cultural heritage of the island. Here are some traditional handicrafts and artwork you can explore in Bali:

Woodcarvings: Balinese woodcarvings are highly regarded and known for their intricate details. You can find a wide range of wooden sculptures depicting various mythological figures, deities, animals, and everyday scenes. Look for skilled craftsmen who create traditional masks, statues, and relief panels using techniques passed down through generations.

Batik and Ikat Textiles: Batik and ikat textiles are traditional Indonesian fabrics that are painstakingly handmade. Batik involves using wax-resistant dyeing techniques to create intricate patterns on cloth, while ikat involves tying and dyeing threads before weaving them. Look for batik and ikat scarves, clothing, tablecloths, wall hangings, and other textile products.

Silver Jewelry: Bali is renowned for its silver jewelry. The traditional Balinese style often incorporates intricate filigree work and detailed designs inspired by nature and Hindu mythology. You can find a wide range of silver jewelry, including earrings, necklaces, bracelets, rings, and decorative items.

Paintings: Balinese paintings are known for their vibrant colors and depiction of mythological and religious themes. The traditional Balinese painting style, often referred to as Kamasan or Ubud style, can be found in galleries and art markets. Look for paintings on canvas or traditional materials such as cotton cloth or palm leaves.

Basketry and Woven Goods: Bali is also known for its basketry and woven goods. You can find baskets made from bamboo, rattan, or other natural materials, as well as woven bags, mats, and other household items. These items are often handmade and feature intricate weaving patterns.

Ceramics and Pottery: Bali has a growing ceramics and pottery scene, with artists creating beautiful pieces using both traditional and contemporary techniques. Look for ceramic bowls, plates, vases, and decorative items adorned with Balinese motifs and colors.

When shopping for traditional handicrafts and artwork, it's always best to support local artisans and purchase from reputable sources. Visit local markets, art galleries, and specialised handicraft shops to find authentic and high-quality pieces. Engage with the artists and craftsmen to learn about their techniques and the stories behind their creations.

Batik and Textiles

Batik and textiles are an integral part of Indonesian culture, and Bali is no exception. The island offers a variety of beautiful batik and textile products that reflect the rich artistic traditions of the region. Here's some information about batik and textiles in Bali:

Batik: Batik is a traditional Indonesian fabric art form that involves the application of wax and dyes to create intricate patterns and designs on cloth. Bali has its own distinct style of batik known as Batik Bali or Batik Tulis Bali. It often features vibrant colors, geometric patterns, and motifs inspired by nature, Hindu mythology, and daily life. Batik can be found in the form of clothing, scarves, wall hangings, tablecloths, and other decorative items.

Ikat: Ikat is another traditional textile technique that is widely practiced in Bali. It involves tying and dyeing the threads before they are woven into fabric, creating intricate and unique patterns. Balinese ikat textiles are known for their vibrant colors and geometric designs. Ikat fabrics are often used to create sarongs, clothing, table runners, and decorative pieces.

Shopping for Batik and Textiles in Bali: To find a wide selection of batik and textiles in

Bali, consider visiting traditional markets, art markets, and specialized textile shops. Here are a few notable places to explore:

1. Sukawati Art Market: Located in Gianyar, near Ubud, Sukawati Art Market is a bustling market known for its wide range of handicrafts, including batik and textiles. It's a great place to find affordable batik clothing, sarongs, and other textile products.

2. Ubud Art Market: While the Ubud Art Market is known for its overall variety of traditional crafts, it also offers a selection of batik and textiles. You can find batik clothing, scarves, and other textile products here.

3. Threads of Life: This ethical gallery and store in Ubud focuses on traditional Indonesian textiles, including batik and ikat. They work directly with weavers and artisans from various regions of Indonesia, including Bali, to promote sustainable

practices and showcase high-quality textiles.

4. Boutique Shops: In the Seminyak and Kuta areas, you'll find boutique shops that offer a curated selection of batik and textiles, often combining traditional techniques with contemporary designs.

When shopping for batik and textiles, examine the quality of the fabric, the intricacy of the patterns, and the overall craftsmanship. Feel free to ask the sellers or artisans about the techniques used and the cultural significance behind the designs. Supporting local artisans and fair trade practices is a great way to appreciate and preserve the traditional art forms of Bali.

Balinese Jewelry and Silverware

Balinese jewelry and silverware are renowned for their intricate designs and craftsmanship. Bali has a long-standing tradition of silverwork, and the island is known for producing stunning jewelry pieces. Here's some information about Balinese jewelry and silverware:

Silver Jewelry: Bali is famous for its silver jewelry, which showcases exquisite designs and traditional craftsmanship. Balinese silver jewelry often incorporates intricate filigree work, granulation (tiny silver beads), and repoussé (raised relief) techniques. The designs are inspired by nature, Hindu mythology, and local cultural motifs. You can find a wide range of silver jewelry in Bali, including earrings, necklaces, bracelets, rings, pendants, and brooches. The jewelry is often made from 925 sterling silver, which is of high quality.

Shopping for Balinese Jewelry: There are several places in Bali where you can find beautiful Balinese silver jewelry. Here are some recommended locations:

1. Celuk Village: Located near Ubud, Celuk Village is renowned for its silver and gold jewelry production. The village is home to numerous workshops and galleries where you can observe the silver-making process and browse a wide range of jewelry designs.

2. Ubud Art Market: While the Ubud Art Market is known for its overall collection of arts and crafts, it also offers a selection of silver jewelry. Many stalls sell intricate silver pieces, allowing you to explore different designs and negotiate prices.

3. Seminyak and Kuta: These popular tourist areas have numerous jewelry boutiques and stores that offer a mix of traditional and contemporary Balinese silver jewelry. Here, you can find unique designs and trendy pieces.

When purchasing Balinese silver jewelry, it's important to ensure the authenticity and quality of the pieces. Look for the 925 sterling silver hallmark, which indicates the purity of the silver. Examine the craftsmanship, detailing, and overall design of the jewelry. Consider buying from reputable stores or directly from silver artisans to support local craftsmanship.

Silverware and Homeware: In addition to jewelry, Bali also produces silverware and homeware items. These include intricately designed silver bowls, plates, utensils, decorative boxes, and other silver-crafted household items. Such pieces can make for unique and elegant souvenirs or home decor.

Whether you're shopping for Balinese jewelry or silverware, take the time to appreciate the craftsmanship and cultural significance behind each piece. Supporting local artisans and purchasing authentic

Balinese silver products not only allows you to take home a beautiful piece of jewelry but also helps sustain the traditional art form and the livelihoods of the craftsmen.

Practical Information and Safety Tips

Health and Safety Considerations

When visiting Bali or any other destination, it's important to prioritize your health and safety. Here are some practical information and safety tips to keep in mind during your visit:

1. Travel Insurance: Before traveling to Bali, ensure that you have comprehensive travel insurance that covers medical emergencies, trip cancellation or delays, and lost or stolen belongings. Check the policy to understand what is included and how to make a claim if needed.

2. Vaccinations and Health Precautions: Consult with your healthcare provider or a travel health clinic well in advance to check if any vaccinations or preventive measures are recommended for your trip to Bali. Common vaccinations for Bali include Hepatitis A and B, typhoid, and tetanus. Consider taking precautions against mosquito-borne diseases like dengue fever by using insect repellents and wearing long sleeves and pants, especially in rural areas.

3. Hygiene and Food Safety: Practice good hygiene by washing your hands regularly, especially before meals. Drink bottled water or ensure that the water has been properly filtered or boiled. Be cautious when consuming street food and choose establishments with good hygiene practices.

4. Sun Protection: Bali has a tropical climate, so protect yourself from the sun's harmful rays by wearing sunscreen (preferably waterproof), a hat, sunglasses,

and lightweight, breathable clothing. Seek shade during the hottest hours of the day and stay hydrated by drinking plenty of water.

5. Traffic and Transportation: Be cautious when crossing the roads in Bali, especially in busy areas. Use designated pedestrian crossings whenever possible. If you're planning to rent a scooter or motorcycle, ensure that you have the necessary license and wear a helmet. Be aware of local traffic rules and drive defensively.

6. Personal Belongings: Keep your personal belongings secure to avoid theft. Use hotel safes or secure lockers when available. Avoid displaying expensive items and be mindful of your surroundings, particularly in crowded places and tourist areas.

7. Emergency Services: Familiarize yourself with local emergency contact numbers, including the local police, ambulance

services, and your embassy or consulate. Keep a copy of important documents such as your passport and travel insurance in a safe place.

8. Natural Disasters: Bali is located in a region prone to natural disasters, such as earthquakes and volcanic activity. Stay informed about the current situation and follow the guidance of local authorities. Register with your embassy or consulate for travel alerts or advisories.

It's always advisable to research and stay updated on the current health and safety guidelines before your trip. Check the travel advisories issued by your government and follow any recommendations or restrictions in place.

By being aware of your surroundings, taking necessary precautions, and practicing common sense, you can have a safe and enjoyable experience during your visit to Bali.

Communication and internet access

in Bali have improved significantly in recent years, making it easier to stay connected during your visit. Here's some information about communication options and internet access in Bali:

1. Mobile Networks: Bali has several mobile network providers that offer SIM cards with voice and data services. You can purchase a prepaid SIM card upon arrival at the airport or from authorized sellers across the island. The major network providers in Bali include Telkomsel, Indosat, XL Axiata, and Three. Ensure that your phone is unlocked and compatible with the local network frequencies.

2. Internet Cafes: Internet cafes can be found in popular tourist areas, allowing you to access the internet and communicate with family and friends. These cafes usually charge an hourly rate for internet usage.

3. Wi-Fi: Most hotels, resorts, cafes, restaurants, and shopping malls in Bali offer Wi-Fi connectivity for their customers. Some establishments may provide complimentary Wi-Fi, while others may require a purchase or provide access codes. The quality and speed of Wi-Fi can vary, so it's advisable to check with the venue beforehand.

4. Mobile Data: With a local SIM card, you can access mobile data and use internet services on your smartphone or other devices. The availability and speed of mobile data coverage may vary in different parts of the island. It's recommended to check the data packages and prices offered by the mobile network providers to find the most suitable option for your needs.

5. Internet Coverage in Remote Areas: While internet access is generally reliable in popular tourist areas, coverage may be limited or slower in more remote or rural parts of Bali. Keep this in mind if you plan to explore off-the-beaten-path areas.

6. Messaging Apps: Utilize messaging apps such as WhatsApp, Viber, or Skype to communicate with family and friends. These apps use internet connectivity, so they can be a cost-effective way to stay in touch without relying solely on cellular services.

7. Virtual Private Network (VPN): If you plan to use public Wi-Fi networks in Bali, consider using a VPN for added security. A VPN encrypts your internet connection and helps protect your personal information from potential hackers.

It's worth noting that network speeds and internet reliability can vary, especially during peak tourist seasons when network congestion may occur. However, overall, staying connected and accessing the internet in Bali is relatively convenient, allowing you to communicate and share your travel experiences with ease.

Etiquette and Cultural Respect

When visiting Bali, it's important to be mindful of the local culture and show respect for Balinese customs and traditions. Here are some etiquette guidelines and cultural considerations to keep in mind:

1. Dress Appropriately: Bali is a predominantly Hindu island, and modest attire is appreciated, especially when visiting temples or religious sites. Both men and women should cover their shoulders and knees. Sarongs are often provided at

temples for visitors to borrow, but it's a good idea to carry your own for convenience.

2. Respect for Temples and Religious Practices: Bali is home to numerous temples and religious sites, which hold great significance to the local community. When visiting temples, dress modestly, remove your shoes before entering, and follow any instructions given by temple staff. Be respectful of religious ceremonies and avoid interrupting or taking photos without permission.

3. Greeting and Politeness: Balinese people are generally warm and friendly. When interacting with locals, it's customary to greet them with a smile and a "hello" or "good day" (Salamat pagi, Salamat siang, Salamat sore). Use "thank you" (Terima kasih) and "you're welcome" (Sama-sama) to express gratitude. Avoid using your left hand for giving or receiving items, as it is considered impolite.

4. Balinese Hierarchy and Respect: Balinese society follows a hierarchical structure based on age, status, and caste. Show respect for elders and those in positions of authority. Use appropriate titles when addressing people, such as "Bapak" (Mr.) and "Ibu" (Mrs.) followed by their name. The Balinese term for "excuse me" is "Permisi."

5. Public Displays of Affection: Balinese culture places modesty and restraint in public behavior. It's advisable to avoid excessive public displays of affection, as it may be seen as inappropriate or disrespectful.

6. Temples and Offerings: When visiting temples or participating in religious ceremonies, avoid touching or stepping on offerings placed on the ground. These offerings are considered sacred. Be mindful not to disturb or damage them.

7. Sacred Sites and Nature: Bali is blessed with beautiful natural landscapes and sacred sites. Show respect for nature and the environment by not littering or damaging natural attractions. Follow designated paths and be mindful of local regulations when exploring natural areas.

8. Balinese Customs and Rituals: Take an interest in and learn about Balinese customs and rituals. Respect and observe local practices, such as joining in traditional ceremonies, being mindful of the noise level during religious events, and seeking permission before entering someone's property or private spaces.

By showing respect for Balinese culture, customs, and traditions, you can create a positive and enriching experience for both yourself and the local community. Remember that cultural sensitivity and an open mind go a long way in fostering meaningful interactions and understanding the local way of life in Bali.

Money-Saving Tips and Bargaining Techniques

When it comes to saving money and bargaining in Bali, here are some tips and techniques to keep in mind:

1. Research and Compare Prices: Before making any purchases, research the average prices of the items you're interested in. This will give you a baseline for negotiation and help you identify if a price is fair or inflated. Compare prices at different shops or markets to get an idea of the general range.

2. Shop at Local Markets: Local markets, such as Ubud Art Market, Sukawati Art Market, and Badung Market, are great places to find unique souvenirs and

handicrafts at reasonable prices. These markets often have a variety of sellers, allowing you to compare prices and potentially negotiate for a better deal.

3. Practise Polite Bargaining: Bargaining is common in Bali, especially at markets and small shops. Approach bargaining with a friendly and respectful attitude. Start by offering a price lower than what you're willing to pay, and allow the seller to counteroffer. Be prepared for some back-and-forth negotiation. Remember to stay polite and maintain a pleasant demeanor throughout the process.

4. Bundle Items: If you plan to buy multiple items from the same vendor, consider asking for a discount when purchasing them together. Sellers may be more willing to offer a better deal when they see a larger sale.

5. Be Willing to Walk Away: If you can't reach an agreement on the price, don't be afraid to walk away. Sometimes, this can prompt the seller to lower their price to secure a sale. However, be mindful of being fair and respectful in your negotiations.

6. Ask Locals for Recommendations: Locals can provide valuable insights on where to find good deals and which places offer reasonable prices. Strike up conversations with locals and ask for their recommendations on shopping locations and bargaining strategies.

7. Avoid Tourist Hotspots: Prices in popular tourist areas, such as Seminyak or Kuta, are often higher due to the demand. Consider venturing to less touristy areas, where prices may be more reasonable and bargaining can be more successful.

8. Check for Quality: While it's tempting to focus solely on the price, also assess the

quality of the item you're interested in. Take the time to examine the craftsmanship, materials used, and any potential flaws. It's better to pay a fair price for a well-made item than to get a cheap product of lower quality.

Remember that bargaining is part of the local culture and can be an enjoyable and interactive experience. However, it's important to find a balance between getting a good deal and ensuring fair compensation for the artisans and sellers. Respect their craft and livelihood while aiming for a mutually satisfactory price.

Conclusion

In conclusion, this comprehensive guide provides a wealth of information for anyone planning a trip to Bali. From understanding the best time to visit and visa requirements to packing essentials and budgeting tips, the guide covers all the necessary aspects of trip planning.

The guide then dives into the various regions of Bali, highlighting the unique attractions and experiences they offer. Whether you're seeking cultural immersion in Ubud, beachside luxury in Seminyak, or adventure in Uluwatu, there's something for everyone in Bali's diverse regions.

The must-visit attractions section showcases the iconic sites, temples, waterfalls, and natural wonders that make Bali so captivating. It encourages travelers to explore the rich cultural heritage and stunning landscapes that the island has to offer.

Food lovers will appreciate the section on Balinese cuisine, which introduces traditional dishes, local food markets, and upscale dining options. It caters to a variety of tastes, including vegetarian and vegan preferences.

For outdoor enthusiasts, the guide presents a range of adventurous activities, from surfing and scuba diving to hiking and yoga retreats. Bali's natural beauty provides ample opportunities to explore and indulge in thrilling outdoor experiences.

The guide also delves into Balinese culture and traditions, shedding light on the arts, temples, dance, music, and vibrant festivals that shape the island's identity. It emphasizes the importance of cultural respect and etiquette when engaging with the local community.

Furthermore, the guide offers insights into shopping and souvenir options, from the vibrant Ubud Art Market to the trendy shopping district of Seminyak. It provides tips for finding unique handicrafts, textiles, jewelry, and silverware, while also sharing money-saving techniques and bargaining tips.

Finally, practical information and safety tips cover health considerations, communication options, and essential etiquette guidelines to ensure a smooth and enjoyable trip to Bali.

Overall, this guide serves as a comprehensive resource, empowering travelers to make informed decisions and create unforgettable experiences in the captivating island paradise of Bali.

Printed in Great Britain
by Amazon